THE ENTREPRENEUR'S GUIDE
TO FINANCIAL WELL-BEING

THE

ENTREPRENEUR'S

GUIDE

TO FINANCIAL WELL-BEING

WAYNE B. TITUS III, CPA/PFS, AIFA®

FOUNDING PARTNER OF AMDG FINANCIAL

LIONCREST
PUBLISHING

THE ENTREPRENEUR'S GUIDE TO FINANCIAL WELL-BEING

ISBN   978-1-5445-1236-5 *Paperback*
       978-1-5445-1237-2 *Ebook*

If you have questions, please contact:

Wayne B. Titus III

218 S. Main Street

Plymouth, Michigan 48170

(734) 737-0866

info@amdgservices.com

More information about this book, as well as additional
resources, can be found at www.WayneBTitus3.com

CONTENTS

FOREWORD

So you're an entrepreneur. You're regarded by others as "the crazy one," the explorer who ventures into uncharted territory. You have the ability to see an opportunity to improve something, while others see only what's broken or missing. You disrupt and shake up the status quo.

Congratulations! Who wouldn't want to be you? You get to set your own office hours and dress code, and design and decorate your own office space. You're accountable to no one.

Best of all, you get to make lots and lots of money. Pretty cool—right?

Not so fast. If you're an entrepreneur, you're different, and that may jeopardize your financial well-being. If you're like most entrepreneurs, you're willing to live on the edge of bankruptcy to feed your "vision."

I was delighted when Wayne invited me to be part of his book. We have known each other for years and share a common sense of purpose and passion for bringing a higher level of integrity and professionalism to the financial services industry. (In addition, we both have ties to Hanover, Pennsylvania.)

For more than three decades, I have focused on advancing the subject of fiduciary responsibility and developing standards for prudent moral and ethical decision making. In 2007, I formed the company 3ethos and began to study the leadership and stewardship behaviors that define the attributes of a trusted financial adviser serving in a fiduciary capacity. More recently, we added to our fiduciary framework groundbreaking research on neuro-leadership. This research identifies the neurological markers (hotspots in the brain) of exemplary leaders. You'll read more about our efforts in this book.

Our research is in behavioral behavioral governance[SM]— defined as the interrelationship between leadership, stewardship, and governance. As it relates to Wayne's work, we believe behavioral governance provides helpful insights in understanding the challenges associated with nudging entrepreneurs to consider their financial well-being. As Wayne points out, that's where an integrative financial adviser can help.

If you're an entrepreneur, you're wired differently. These differences contribute to your success, but they can also contribute to your downfall financially. You need to gain a deeper understanding and appreciation of the fact that financial well-being has a direct impact on your "vision." Taking a famous line from the movie *The Right Stuff*—"No bucks, no Buck Rogers."

When it comes to choosing the right adviser, you're in good hands with Wayne's guidance. His book arms you with everything you need to know. The next step is up to you.

—DON TRONE, L5, GFS®, CEO, 3ETHOS

INTRODUCTION

Life moves at warp speed for most entrepreneurs, and if you're like many of my clients, you face challenges on a regular basis. Common everyday pains include the following:

- Your spouse doesn't understand your business decisions. Perhaps she or he believes your choices are too risky, when in fact, you are trying to capitalize on opportunities, such as the chance to buy your building at far below its value from a motivated seller.
- You struggle with not knowing what your responsibility is to your employees and what is best for them. You'd like to help them save for retirement, but you're uncertain how far you should go to be impactful.
- You feel overwhelmed by business growth and lost when it comes to the tension of bringing in sufficient

profits and minimizing taxes. You may feel as if you receive a lack of comprehensive advice from your CPA. Meanwhile, your spouse might be pressuring you to sell the business because it takes all your time.

I understand these challenges because I've experienced them myself as an entrepreneur. I know what it feels like to leave behind a steady paycheck and work in a tiny office where you're the one paying for the office supplies and the electricity. I know the pressure of having your family dependent on your venture succeeding. As an entrepreneur, I've found ways to scale and manage wealth using prudent investment strategies. I've minimized my tax burden to the highest extent possible. As of this writing, I've worked with hundreds of entrepreneurs and their families, successfully helping them manage their wealth and plan wisely for the future.

MY BACKGROUND

Every entrepreneur lives, breathes, and eats his or her business, and I understand that perfectly because I come from an entrepreneurial family. My dad owned a Cadillac/Oldsmobile dealership when I was growing up. He worked at least seventy hours a week, every day but Sunday, often not returning home until late at night. When I was younger, I'd go out to breakfast with my dad every Saturday at the Sunnyside Diner in Hanover,

Pennsylvania. That was my big day with him because of his schedule. I began working for my dad when I was eight years old. I started off in his dealership washing cars—over the years I washed thousands of them. I swept the body shop and became a mechanic's apprentice. I became a salesman at seventeen; later, I moved into the finance and insurance department, helping customers with contracts. Eventually, I became sales manager and then general manager.

I learned the value of hard work and integrity from my dad, and he learned it from my grandfather, who grew up on a farm in rural northeastern Pennsylvania and became a real estate developer in Harrisburg, Pennsylvania. (My great-grandfather, Clarence, a farmer and eventually a county clerk, was known to have said after church on Sunday, "Visiting friends and family will not help the potatoes grow.") From both my dad and my grandfather, I also learned that when you're an entrepreneur, there's almost never a division between work and family. It all merges together, and while work-life balance is always a goal, it rarely happens. You do the best you can.

Meanwhile, entrepreneurs tend to be stubborn, independent, and a little hardheaded—more than a little, in fact. But you have to be hardheaded to go your own way because so many people will tell you you're crazy. In 2002, I struck out on my own to assist entrepreneurs in wealth management and planning, founding AMDG Financial and AMDG Business Advisory Services. The stock market had recently collapsed. The economy was in deep trouble. When I told people I was leaving my secure job as a senior manager at a large accounting firm to become an entrepreneur, they nodded their heads politely and said, "That's great." But I saw in their eyes what they were really thinking: "This guy is nuts!" According to experts and every economic barometer, it was not the time to go into the financial services industry. But it didn't matter to me what the market was doing, because I was convinced that the opportunities were there.

I was inspired to become a CPA after seeing my dad receive poor business advice from his accountant. My education and professional experience reinforced the lesson I learned from my dad's problems: entrepreneurs must possess the right information if they are to make wise business decisions, and they need excellent advisers to help them.

I worked for Ernst & Young, and then Coopers & Lybrand. My client base primarily consisted of small entrepreneurial clients for whom I performed financial audits and systems audits. When Coopers & Lybrand merged with Price Waterhouse, I continued to move up the ranks, working with Fortune 50 companies like Ford, Visteon, and Caterpillar. I got the itch to strike out on my own in 2002. It wasn't because I lacked opportunities, but because I wanted what many entrepreneurs want: independence, flexibility, and, most important, the chance to make a significant impact on people's lives and find the time to contribute to society. I decided to integrate tax, financial, and investment strategies for families and small businesses with two practices: a tax-and-accounting practice and a wealth management one.

I started my two companies in a six-by-eight-foot office that I had to enter sideways to have any hope of maneuvering around my desk. Today we've grown to a firm of eleven people managing $150 million in assets (as of the end of July 2018). Success has come from hard work and the determination to always do the right things for our clients. People told me it took guts to leave a solid corporate career for an entrepreneurial one, but what I did is consistent with what the entrepreneurs I serve do every day. They see a gap into which they can insert themselves and their skills, using it not just for their benefit, but also for the benefit of those around them.

TAKE A LOOK AT THE FUTURE

I'd like to ask you now to picture yourself in the future, somewhere between two and five years from today. See yourself as experiencing a high level of well-being around your finances. Everything isn't perfect—because nothing ever is—but you're not in a state of constant worry. You don't get stressed when you hear news reports about the stock market's ups and downs or the volatility of the economy. In this future, you have the financial means to take vacations with your family, making wonderful memories, or to do anything else you value without fear or guilt. Even if this future scene doesn't seem possible because of the current state of your finances, I'm here to tell you it is.

Rick, for example, weathered a major storm and came out the other side. A decade ago, he went bankrupt from an entrepreneurial venture and fell into a serious depression that took months to navigate. Eventually, he met a fellow through a social services organization who was looking for a succession candidate for his small retail business. Rick and his wife ended up buying it. Life was looking up, but Rick felt increasingly uncomfortable with his financial adviser. (The term *adviser* should be used loosely because the guy was more of a straight broker.) When Rick told him he wanted to reassess the current financial strategy for his new business, the broker's response was "It's my way or the highway." That's when Rick came to me, seeking additional financial information.

As Rick went through my process, I saw that his retirement plan for his employees wasn't benefiting them or him to the highest extent possible. I revised his 401(k) profit-sharing plan and integrated it with a pension plan. Now he and his wife shelter $250,000 to $300,000 of income each year. They save federal, state, and payroll taxes on that amount and provide the best benefits possible to their employees, all without going broke in the process. One way I help them do that is by minimizing the impact of taxes through various strategies. That savings has freed Rick up to fulfill other passions, such as his desire to be more charitable. Rick, who has been deeply involved with Rotary International for most of his adult life, now supports critical projects that provide clean water and maternal healthcare in developing countries.

Rick's future was achieved through what I call Fiduciary GPS^{SM}; it is a plan my team and I believe can help any entrepreneur move toward a brighter future. I will discuss it in far more detail in Chapter 3, but in brief, Fiduciary GPS^{SM} is a process in which I gather (1) the coordinates of where you are now and (2) your desired financial destination. Then I create a master map that documents the known obstacles and sets a course we will navigate together. From checkpoint to checkpoint, we adjust our course based on how things look on the ground, the terrain ahead, and the direction you want to go. Ultimately, your course depends on the obstacles you face and the summits you want to achieve. Just like having GPS in your car, this process provides security and a sense of relief. You are assured you won't get lost. You know you are heading in the right direction for your and your family's future. For me, serving you means serving your family.

WHAT A TRUSTWORTHY ADVISER IS AND WHY YOU NEED ONE

What I've learned from working with hundreds of entrepreneurs is that when it comes to finances, they often don't know what they don't know. I've discovered that entrepreneurs need a great CPA and a trustworthy financial adviser. It's best if both roles are accomplished by one individual. Working with two different people is possible, but coordination is absolutely essential to keep critical information from falling through the cracks.

One of the most important things I want you to take away from *The Entrepreneur's Guide to Financial Well-Being* is what I mean by the word *trustworthy* in reference to a financial adviser. Trustworthiness is not likability. It is not friendship. It is not a reputation based on a referral from a friend, boss, relative, or coworker. By trustworthy adviser, I mean an adviser who isn't considering his or her wallet when offering guidance: a person who always puts the client's agenda first. Unfortunately, the way advisers receive compensation in the financial services industry is confusing for even the smartest entrepreneur. Transparency about how advice relates to receiving commissions on products is often lacking. (I'll discuss this in more detail in Chapter 2.) It's true that some financial advisers are required to put their clients' best interests before their own because of the "fiduciary standard" established under the Investment Advisers Act of 1940. However, that standard only applies to certain types of advisers in specific situations, all of which the layperson is usually unaware. I started my own practice to ensure that I could not only adhere to the fiduciary standard in all aspects of my business but go beyond it whenever possible and always deal with my clients with integrity and clarity.

If you are like most entrepreneurs, your business is your passion. You work all the time, even though it doesn't necessarily feel like work. Your attention is focused on solving problems, and even crises, on a day-to-day basis. That's also why you need a trustworthy financial adviser. Just because you're an entrepreneur doesn't mean you're equipped to deal with complex financial arenas such as employee benefits, strategic tax management, financial statements, cash flow, and so forth. Financial literacy is still rarely taught in our educational system. In addition, as an entrepreneur, it is easy to become isolated. You bear the burden of leadership: aloneness. It can be difficult to talk over challenges with friends or your spouse because they might not understand or be able to help. A trustworthy adviser does everything possible to ensure that you aren't taken advantage of and that you don't succumb to a quick fix. He or she also provides an objective picture around your finances, filtering out the media noise about the day-to-day economy. By doing so, the adviser helps you reduce your chances of making an emotional decision based on information that doesn't apply to you.

Let's look at two additional aspects a trustworthy adviser possesses: "eptitude" and a strong process.

"EPTITUDE" OVER APTITUDE

The concept of "eptitude" comes from *New Yorker* staff writer and surgeon Atul Gawande's book *The Checklist Manifesto*. This seminal work outlines the importance of checklists in ensuring that surgeons and other professionals avoid devastating errors. Even surgeons with a high aptitude—the natural ability of a person to be able to accomplish a certain skillset—might be inept. That is, they have blind spots, or things they miss, especially when the systems they deal with are complex and interdependent. When that happens, aptitude doesn't matter. You can't implement what's needed in your profession if your "eptitude" is deficient. Checklists help ensure eptitude.

Finding a trustworthy adviser requires due diligence on your part. As an accountant, when I perform an audit, I must ask for evidence so I don't unduly rely on information that turns out to be inaccurate. Yet when entrepreneurs are referred to a financial adviser by, say, a friend or an associate, they often don't ask for enough evidence to discover whether that adviser is the right one for them and their circumstances. That adviser may have investment and financial aptitude, and even a level of aptitude related to understanding tax implications. But how do you know they have the "eptitude" for your situation as an entrepreneur? What evidence can they provide to demonstrate that they understand complexity and that their process considers that complexity and provides integration? As an entrepreneur, achieving financial success is interdependent on many variables, including tax, financial, and investment strategy. Often, I meet entrepreneurs who have been using the same adviser for years, but he or she is no longer helpful or strategic. Or the adviser lacks the vision to see what you will need down the road with your business and your life. In either circumstance, undue reliance on an adviser who doesn't know how to navigate your world can be disastrous.

If you're confident you have the right adviser, your well-being is likely to rise. How can you tell? One way is to rate your position. In the excellent book *Wellbeing: The Five Essential Elements*, authors Tom Rath and Jim Harter ask you to put yourself on what's called a Cantril Scale, a metaphorical ladder with rungs numbered from zero to ten. Zero represents the worst possibilities of life, ten the best. You're asked to identify which step of the ladder you believe you're on in different areas, including financial well-being. This exercise can be a good start, but my desire is for you to take such a question further. I'd like you to understand that your perception of your financial well-being may not be your reality. I want you to clearly identify not only where you are financially but also where you could be if you challenged the status quo.

The only way to challenge the status quo is to ask for evidence and, if that evidence cannot be presented, have the courage to seek out and choose a financial adviser who can point out your blind spots. Even if you think you don't have any blind spots, you probably do. People tend to be unaware of gaps in their knowledge base, as demonstrated by a psychological model called the Johari window. Take a look at the following diagram and see if it looks familiar:

JOHARI WINDOW

	KNOWN TO SELF	UNKNOWN TO SELF
KNOWN TO OTHERS	**Open/Public** *(known by self and others)*	**Blind Spot** *(unknown by self, but known by others)*
UNKNOWN TO OTHERS	**Hidden Area** *(hidden by self, but kept unknown by others)*	**Unknown** *(by self and others)*

In the upper-left window, you put information that is known to both yourself and others. The window below it represents information you withhold from others, often for good reason. The upper-right quadrant represents your blind spots, the aspects and information others see and know about you that you do not. Finally, the lower-right represents what is hidden from both the self and others.

Entrepreneurs like to go with their gut feelings. They're mold breakers. But when you collaborate with a trustworthy adviser, allowing them to share their observations and challenge your perceptions, you have an opportunity to obtain feedback and evidence for those intuitive decisions. You're not relying solely on how you feel or on what you think you know.

WITH A TRUSTWORTHY ADVISER, PROCESS IS CRUCIAL

Your financial well-being is a big-picture scenario. All the moving parts need to work together. My goal is for you to understand the following:

- High-performing advisers have strong processes in place to identify and understand your needs, and they monitor those processes to make needed adjustments.
- You can pick the best adviser by ascertaining whether those processes line up with your particular situation.

- That adviser should provide a great deal of clarity about what you can expect from the relationship. In addition, he or she should be skilled and confident in connecting your business growth with integrated and holistic wealth management that includes tax, financial, and investment strategies.

It's important to understand that a good process informs strategies, which determine tactics. If, instead, tactics drive strategies, you end up cobbling together a process that eventually suffers under its own weight. That's when you find yourself in a reactive mode, not a proactive one.

In *The Checklist Manifesto*, Gawande stresses the importance of taking a proactive approach to complex tasks; that's why checklists work—they ensure you're doing the most important things, even when the situation is complex and chaotic. It's true in the operating room and in the cockpit: every time a pilot readies for takeoff, he or she goes through a checklist. If an emergency occurs, he or she immediately consults another checklist. The complexity of both situations requires that nothing be missed. Otherwise, the outcome could produce fatalities.

In the same way, an excellent holistic wealth management process will help you avoid financial "fatalities" and free you up to pursue what's most meaningful to you. In my experience, entrepreneurs are often superior at optimizing systems and processes to create solutions, more than most people. This book is designed to provide the insight for you to optimize your financial well-being. As you read on, you will learn more about the importance of process in your relationship with an adviser. You'll also be educated on the aspects of a well-coordinated plan and wealth management techniques. In the next chapter, we'll discuss the emotional journey an entrepreneur often takes and how to reduce complexity by finding a trustworthy adviser.

PART ONE

YOU, THE ENTREPRENEUR

CHAPTER ONE

AN EMOTIONAL JOURNEY

Edie jumped into the entrepreneurial life hoping to gain more flexibility with her schedule and more time with her kids as they entered the wild and woolly territory of their teenage years. Yet here she was, almost as exhausted as she had been working for a high-powered management consulting firm and traveling hundreds of hours a year.

Edie was an MIT graduate; she knew how to work and work hard. Her brilliance was unquestionable. When she decided to strike out on her own, creating customer relationship management (CRM) systems for small businesses in the Detroit area, she had known it wasn't going to be easy at first; still, she had been so unfulfilled and unappreciated at her corporate job, she had thought the change was worth the risk. But at forty-three, Edie was exhausted from trying to figure out how to manage the financial aspects of running a company and bewildered by the complexity of her personal wealth management situation.

The first several years had been uncomplicated because her startup had run at a loss and she didn't owe any taxes. But now, at year five, the company was experiencing rapid growth. Edie didn't have time to educate herself on what she needed to do on the business side to manage her tax bill. All of a sudden, Edie was netting $500,000 a year, and her federal tax bill was a whopping $143,000. That was more in taxes than Edie had ever paid.

As so many entrepreneurs know, once your company starts to scale, things tend to get out of control. Edie's biggest expense was payroll, which was running about $30,000 a month, not including her own salary. Edie found herself working until three, four, even five in the morning, putting together proposals for project bids. It didn't stop there. Once the company won a project, it was always a crunch to meet deadlines. Edie's family time was shrinking fast.

Edie's husband, Frank, was fifty and had worked for GM for over twenty-five years. He had been looking forward to slowing down. But Edie's widowed mother, Vivian, had been diagnosed with dementia a year prior, and Frank now found himself taking on more and more of Vivian's care while Edie tried to keep all the balls in the air at work. Frank had been considering early retirement, but he was worried that was going to be impossible if Edie's firm floundered. Meanwhile, Frank didn't understand many of Edie's financial decisions. In bed at night, all Frank could think about was the family's finances. Their taxes were higher because they were in a higher bracket. They had student loan debt from when Edie had gone back for her MBA. There was credit card debt. Plus, they needed to save for their two daughters' college educations. For three decades, Frank had been steadily putting money away into his 401(k). Edie had been more sporadic in the past several years because of the task of getting her business off the ground. The couple did possess several financial products purchased early in their marriage, but Frank constantly worried their savings would not amount to enough for a comfortable retirement.

Both Frank and Edie wanted to do what was best for their family's financial future and help Edie's business thrive. However, they were unsure how to manage it all. Everything felt overwhelming.

A DIFFICULT PATH

This might not be your exact situation, but portions of it likely ring true for you. Forging an entrepreneurial path is tough. Your friends aren't on the same journey, and your spouse may be simultaneously supportive and stressed (and even wary) regarding your choices. As an entrepreneur, you face isolation, self-doubt, and a thousand questions a day around running your business, never mind how to manage your finances. Financial stress is the biggest area of conflict in a committed relationship because it triggers our fight-or-flight response, the conditioning that kicks in when we fear for our safety. Financial problems also impact an entire family.

As humans, we often hope to find a quick fix to get ourselves out of a financially troubling and stressful situation. One of the best things you can do is find a financial adviser who understands that your personal life is intertwined with your business. An adviser who views your finances from this standpoint will place you in a process that will immediately begin to relieve your pressure. Inside such a framework, you can see fear for what it is: an emotion, not a real-life scenario. A clear process orients you; it makes opportunities visible. It allows you to know exactly where you are and what you can expect moving forward.

THE DANGER OF NORMALIZING FINANCIAL STRESS

The entrepreneurial personality is a reactive one. An effective financial adviser takes the opposite approach, balancing your tendency to focus on putting out fires or search for a quick solution. Without that opposing view challenging you, your head is, unfortunately, likely to stay in the sand.

In addition, entrepreneurs often normalize a high degree of financial stress. They get on autopilot and lose interest in addressing the pain because it's too distracting from the day-to-day challenges of keeping a business and a family running. The danger is that compound stress can threaten your relationships and your health. Yet the more stressful finances are to think about, the more entrepreneurs tend to disregard them. The more they disregard them, the more stressful finances become. This dog-chasing-its-own-tail cycle most often occurs when a business grows more and more successful and the entrepreneur is tempted to rationalize that everything is great, so it's OK to put finances on the back burner.

However, as Edie and Frank discovered, one of the problems success brings is higher taxes. When you have a tax adviser who only does two things—prepares a tax return and addresses business compliance issues—you rarely get the opportunity to minimize your taxes. At tax time, such an adviser simply reports what you owe and why. They don't propose a process for addressing the future.

A trustworthy adviser, however, looks at the big picture. In doing so, he or she won't add more complexity to your life. You won't be required to know every detail of wealth management and planning. Instead, you'll be provided with clarity on strategy and direction. You will receive information that is easy to digest. As a result, you will also be able to understand your options and choose, with confidence, what is best for yourself and your family.

THE PROBLEM WITH UNDUE RELIANCE

An entrepreneur can also be lulled into a false sense of security around her finances if she has a good cash flow and is paying debt down systematically. It's critical that you not rely on your gut or a false sense of security around your personal finances or those of your business, because financial security is relative. Your spouse may feel that you need to be saving more and paying down debt. Even if markets are going up, your tax bill may not be going down. It's essential you don't believe everything will somehow work out once you sell your company in a successful exit strategy. Any uninformed perspectives you hold constitute undue reliance.

Instead of going with your gut, you need an adviser who can guide and educate you on the best route forward, helping you design a strategy for the next five or six years, or more. He or she should (gently) challenge your status quo. For instance, ever since the US tax laws changed in January 2018, we began to alter the tax plan structures of individuals and entrepreneurs filing jointly, and to provide potential opportunities for tax savings and added tax credits for our clients. Any adviser you use should do the same. A decent financial plan can often be transformed into a good one, and a good one can be made great when combined with a prudent investment strategy and an integrated tax and cash flow plan. With the right adviser, you'll gain clarity and confidence in your financial decision making. The next chapter discusses how to find that person.

CHAPTER TWO

ENGAGING THE RIGHT ADVISER FOR YOU

Mandy is an engineer in her midfifties who owns a small manufacturing company that performs 3D printing. The company's primary business is providing parts to automotive companies. Mandy's company has been fairly successful the past fifteen years, even through the recession. Yet Mandy senses she is in over her head when it comes to her company's finances, especially around reducing her tax burden. She also feels adrift in growing her own wealth.

Her biggest challenge with her company has been keeping the right people. Mandy would like to try to share some of her profits with her employees as incentives and help them save for retirement. However, she doesn't have a profit-sharing vehicle or a retirement plan in place for employees or for herself. She does have an IRA left over from a corporate job she had in her twenties and thirties. That portfolio has had good returns over time, but Mandy often thinks those returns could be even better. Mandy isn't sure how to find the right adviser. She's heard horror stories about people getting ripped off by financial advisers and brokers and doesn't want that to happen to her. As a result, Mandy has done nothing, which she knows isn't a good move either.

MODELS OF FINANCIAL SERVICE

Mandy is like numerous entrepreneurs I encounter. She feels embarrassed about her lack of knowledge about the financial industry. Yet the truth is, the way the industry works is confusing for many people. There are different models and different levels of responsibility to the client. Here are the three models, all of which are tied to compensation:

Which Hat Does Your Adviser Wear?
Compensation Structures and Duties of Care to Clients

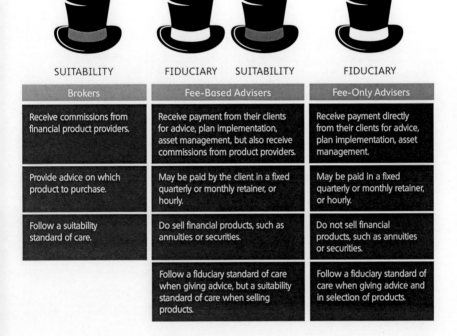

SUITABILITY	FIDUCIARY	SUITABILITY	FIDUCIARY
Brokers	**Fee-Based Advisers**		**Fee-Only Advisers**
Receive commissions from financial product providers.	Receive payment from their clients for advice, plan implementation, asset management, but also receive commissions from product providers.		Receive payment directly from their clients for advice, plan implementation, asset management.
Provide advice on which product to purchase.	May be paid by the client in a fixed quarterly or monthly retainer, or hourly.		May be paid in a fixed quarterly or monthly retainer, or hourly.
Follow a suitability standard of care.	Do sell financial products, such as annuities or securities.		Do not sell financial products, such as annuities or securities.
	Follow a fiduciary standard of care when giving advice, but a suitability standard of care when selling products.		Follow a fiduciary standard of care when giving advice and in selection of products.

- **Securities brokers and insurance agents** receive compensation by the commissions they earn from selling financial products, such as stocks, bonds, annuities, or other investments.
- **Fee-based advisers** receive compensation by earning a percentage of the assets they manage or a quarterly or monthly retainer. They may also be compensated on an hourly basis. A good way to remember how fee-based advisers work is this: they receive fees when providing advice on allocation. Allocation is

percentage of equity versus fixed income in a portfolio. In addition, fee-based advisers almost always receive commissions when selecting a product for your portfolio.

- **Fee-only advisers** are compensated directly by their clients for advice, implementation of their financial plans, and asset management. Similar to fee-based advisers, they can be paid through a percentage of assets or retainer, or on an hourly basis. They provide advice on allocation and on selecting investments. They don't sell financial products and consequently don't receive a commission from product providers.

To understand the financial services industry's models of legal responsibility, it is important to know a brief history of finance:

The 1939 Securities and Exchange Act created the role of brokers. The act says that if a broker sells a product and receives commission, a license is required (of which there are several types). A year later, the Investment Advisers Act of 1940 came around, which states that a financial professional must possess a separate license to give financial advice to clients, and if that advice refers to a specific product, the adviser is not permitted to receive a commission. Securities brokers primarily deal in transactions, while advisers are more focused on relationships.

Two different standards govern the work of financial advisers and securities brokers. For registered investment advisers, the fiduciary standard dictates that the adviser will do what is in the best interest of the client at all times. In short, a fiduciary must be loyal to the client first, not to his or her wallet. Securities brokers, on the other hand, have to fulfill what is called the suitability standard, meaning that they believe whatever they recommend to their clients is "suitable" for them (the standard for insurance agents is similar). Because the word *suitability* has a ring of trust and authenticity, many people don't understand there's a big difference between the suitability standard and the fiduciary one. The medical industry has one standard: "Do no harm." But the financial world has two, and the majority of the public doesn't know that the suitability rule is a lower standard of care.

If you grew up, like I did, in the era of *Schoolhouse Rock*—those animated, educational short films on Saturday mornings between cartoons—you might remember the song about the Latin phrases *caveat emptor* and *caveat venditor*. *Caveat emptor* means "let the buyer beware," while *caveat venditor* is "let the seller beware." The suitability standard comes down to *caveat emptor*—buyer beware. It would make little sense to go to a doctor who followed a standard of care that stated "Try not to harm."

FEE-BASED ADVISERS STRADDLE TWO STANDARDS

Things get complex with a fee-based adviser. When the adviser offers guidance in areas such as asset allocation, he or she is held to the fiduciary standard. But when the conversation moves toward recommending specific products in a client's portfolio (which they are also licensed to sell and receive commissions for), they switch hats and become securities brokers or insurance agents. Now, they must meet only the suitability standard. In plain terms, fee-based advisers split their duties and bifurcate their responsibilities. But clients almost never know when such financial professionals make the switch or what difference it makes. They're left, instead, with the nagging feeling that something's off, though they can't quite put their finger on what happened. It's a common blind spot for people who use fee-based financial advisers.

For example, Mark is an entrepreneur who expressed concern to his fee-based adviser about downside market risk. They discussed allocation for a while, and then the adviser recommended a variable indexed annuity product with a ten-year schedule. At a cost of $200,000, it sounded reasonable to Mark, who didn't realize the adviser was recommending a ten-year schedule because he received a significant up-front commission on the sale and $1,000 in fees per year for the next decade. The adviser's recommendations likely earned him $30,000. Any additional investment, tax, or financial advice will cost Mark extra.

If, in year two, Mark decides he wanted to get out of the product, he has to pay 9 percent of the value ($18,000) to do so, called a surrender charge. Meanwhile, because of the way the contract was written, Mark remains unaware of the original up-front commission, which is nonreturnable. He won't get it back, because he's broken the contract.

As you can see, getting out of these kinds of products can be financially devastating. Disclosures should be clearly explained to clients up front, but they are not. Meanwhile, fee-based advisers market with language that preys on their clients' fears about financial stability. Remember, fee-based advisers only have to demonstrate that these products are "suitable," but not necessarily in a client's best interest.

A fee-only adviser, however, abides by the fiduciary standard, never accepting commission. The fiduciary standard applies to both aspects of the adviser-client conversation—first, the adviser provides guidance on asset allocation, such as what percentage of a portfolio should be in equity versus fixed income, based on a client's preferred strategy. Second, he or she provides advice on selecting products. If Mark had seen a fee-only adviser, a variable indexed annuity likely would not have been recommended, because it wouldn't have been considered in his best interest. Instead, the fee-only adviser might have recommended structuring a portfolio of low-cost, institutional, and well-diversified mutual funds. On such a portfolio, Mark would have paid no up-front commission and roughly $3,600 a year, consisting of a roughly 1.80 percent asset management fee and .30 percent mutual fund administration fee. These costs would also include the cost of ongoing advice for integrating tax, financial, and investment strategies.

MY PATH: FEE-ONLY

Fee-based advisers comprise the fastest-growing area of the financial services industry. I don't believe a fee-based adviser will intentionally hurt a client. I am not denigrating the entire sector. I simply want you to know that they wear two hats, and the suitability standard means they are not necessarily going to scour the marketplace for the best product for you, nor do they have the legal responsibility to do so.

When I struck out on my own, I decided to do so as a fee-only adviser. I wanted to focus only on what was best for my clients. As a CPA, it was critical for me to be independent in both fact and appearance. I never wanted my clients wondering why I was making a recommendation or whether I was going to be compensated for it. If you have a trustworthy relationship with a fee-based adviser, my intention is not to disrupt it. But in addition to the transparency issue, I want you to be aware that a fee-based adviser doesn't necessarily provide the kind of guidance from which an entrepreneur benefits, one that selects products and integrates tax, financial, and investment strategies that are purely in your best interest according to the fiduciary standard.

A STANDARD OF BEHAVIORS

Understanding compensation and responsibility models is critical in evaluating a potential adviser—the more you know about how they make their money and their legal responsibility to you, the better. Another important consideration is whether the adviser or firm has strong processes in place.

You can assess this by looking at their behaviors, the key drivers of a strong process. You need to know: Does this adviser possess the right behaviors, and are they consistently demonstrated? If so, he or she is adhering to what is known as behavioral governance. It is a new body of research that examines the interrelationships between a key decision maker's leadership, stewardship, and governance. The research is being led by the Connecticut-based company 3ethos, which was founded by Don Trone. Trone is regarded as the "Father of Fiduciary." The other 3ethos cofounders include Rear Admiral Steve Branham (US Coast Guard, retired); Sean

Hannah, PhD, Wake Forest University School of Business (US Army, retired colonel); John Sumanth, PhD, Wake Forest University School of Business; and Mary Lou Wattman.

Hannah and his team have conducted groundbreaking research in the field of neuro-leadership. The neuroscientists have discovered that exemplary leaders possess six distinct neurological markers:

- Procedural justice: The capacity for ethical leadership, particularly the ability to enact a fair, just, and transparent process to resolve moral conflicts or to allocate limited resources.
- Vision/Inspiration: The capacity for transformative leadership, including the ability to connect with others and provide shared visions and strategies that engage, gain commitment and alignment, and inspire higher levels of performance.
- Self-complexity: A leader's capacity to understand his or her own self-worth within changing roles and requirements, as well as the ability to adjust and adapt thoughts and behaviors to enact more appropriate responses to ill-defined, changing, and evolving situations.
- Situational awareness: The capacity to perceive changes in the environment, interpret those changes to determine whether and how they may impact

goals and objectives, and make predictions as to how changes may impact future events.

- Executive control: The capacity to resolve conflicts between selfish, impulsive desires and adherence to a goal with a higher order to benefit the greater good.
- Social astuteness: The capacity for social intelligence, interpersonal influence, the ability to network, and sincerity.

In turn, these six neurological markers underpin ten neurological and psychological behaviors that amplify and improve a prudent decision-making process. We associate these behaviors with leadership, stewardship, and governance:

- Leadership is the capacity to inspire and engage others. Leaders are courageous, competent, compassionate, character-full, and collaborative.
- Stewardship is the passion and discipline required to protect the long-term interests of others. Excellent stewards are aligned, adaptive, attentive, accountable, and authentic.
- Governance is the ability to manage a prudent decision-making process based on the best interest of those served, as well as the best practices and generally accepted principles of the industry.

Whether a financial professional possesses these markers and how well they are developed impacts his or her ability to make prudent decisions and implement a strong process. Let's take Bernie Madoff as an example. The Audible series on Madoff, *Ponzi Supernova*, as well as the *New York Times* bestseller *No One Would Listen: A True Financial Thriller* (by Harry Markopolos) made it clear to me that Madoff's brain was wired for fraud. Evaluating his actions through a behavioral governance framework, Madoff lacked the neurological capacity for moral and ethical decision making.

We'll go into far more detail in Chapter 6, but, in short, when evaluating a financial adviser, look for someone who demonstrates a capacity to serve in a leadership and stewardship role and who uses a prudent decision-making process grounded in best practices.

Behavioral Governance is the study of leadership (the ability to inspire and engage), stewardship (the ability to preserve and protect over the long-term and the ability to manage a prudent process to achieve the goals and objectives of the stakeholders).

Entrepreneurs often find themselves in complex financial situations where things can't turn on a dime. Yet in business, change can happen quickly. Being nimble doesn't mean you make uninformed decisions or those inconsistent with your behavior; it does mean that you have a strong behavioral foundation and a process in place to be sure you consider the most important information *before* a decision. Changing tactics without considering the full impact can lead to business disaster. In baseball, the coach doesn't change his lineup in the middle of the game. He might tweak it, but he has a strategy and he sticks to it.

Working with an adviser who is grounded in behavioral governance, and who possesses a strong process that informs strategy and tactics, is essential. As an entrepreneur, your financial strategy must be deliberately and patiently created. Otherwise, you will lose your sense of financial well-being.

LOOK FOR MORE THAN INVESTMENT CONSULTING

As I said in the introduction, entrepreneurs often don't know what they don't know. And there is a lot to know, because most entrepreneurs have far different financial situations than those with regular, salaried jobs. Yet most advisers provide only investment consulting. Entrepreneurs need more. A financial professional suitable for an entrepreneur should ask such questions as: What was your objective in setting up the company? Was it just to have an exit strategy sale? Was it to provide a service to your clients on an ongoing basis, and then to ensure that continued as your legacy? Do you want to help your employees save for retirement, and how? Who, if anyone, are you grooming to take over your business?

Many first-time entrepreneurs take on the mantle of leadership without being aware of everything that comes with it. When they do become aware of the financial complexity of running a company, the first thing they want to do is solve problems fast. Sometimes they reach for a quick fix. For example, payroll companies often provide cookie-cutter retirement plans to entrepreneurs looking to help employees and themselves with savings goals. Later, those plans can turn out to be expensive and poorly run. Because of one bad experience, an entrepreneur can then become reluctant to consider providing employee benefits.

A benefits plan that is well thought out starts with answering questions such as: Why are you doing it? What's important about it? Do you understand the impacts of the costs on the participants and the plan sponsor? Is it the right design for you and your employees? If the economy goes in a different direction, does it tie you to costs you might not be willing to incur? What's the level of flexibility? What are the limits for owners' contributions? Would they be better off with a different plan? Can more assets be sheltered from taxes with a combination plan?

In addition, your adviser should address your personal goals by gathering critical information used to develop wealth enhancement, wealth transfer, wealth protection, and charitable gifting strategies. We'll discuss all these components in detail in Part 3.

MOVING FROM A MASTER-BUILDER MINDSET

An adviser who can go beyond investment consulting has to have a very different mindset than the average adviser. The shift is very like what Atul Gawande describes in *The Checklist Manifesto*. It's a move from a master-builder mindset to a collaborative one. In premodern times, massive structures such as the great cathedrals of Europe were built at the instruction of a master builder, a person who held all the necessary knowledge in his head. The master builder directed huge teams, but the projects were not collaborative. Today, when a skyscraper is built, there's no master builder. Instead, an integrated team of architects, engineers, and others works together, in constant communication. They establish guideposts and checkpoints along the way to ensure they don't miss anything and the building doesn't contain serious design flaws, such as a foundation that will collapse in an earthquake.

Medicine, Gawande writes, has moved from a master-builder model to one of immense complexity. The financial services industry is on the cusp of a similar shift, which means entrepreneurs should prepare to abandon the idea that they can find one perfect adviser—with all the knowledge in his or her head—and instead adopt a collaborative mindset. It's not always easy to recognize this need, because the financial services industry perpetuates the myth that you can find a master builder to handle all of your challenges.

It's necessary, though. We're living in a time of incredible change, where old structures are disintegrating. Sometimes we fall back on a master-builder mentality just because that's how we've been operating for thousands of years. But that mentality is no longer viable for our time. It is a bridge collapsing under the weight of the past. You can base your decisions on chance, or you can base them on intention. As an entrepreneur, ask yourself: Am I working with a master builder when it comes to my finances? Or am I working with a collaborative, well-designed, and intentional team structure designed to support the weight of the complexity of today's environment?

CHAPTER THREE

FIDUCIARY GPS^{SM}

Any collaborative process is, by definition, complex. It requires standards and specifications that enable team members to make sure everything is done and done well, and properly communicated to other team members. The process must be followed.

When a process fails, goals aren't met, or worse. For example, millions of airbags made by the Japanese firm Takata are under recall because of design flaws. Some bags have exploded, injuring and even killing drivers. The International Organization for Standardization (ISO) creates specifications for manufacturing. Takata was likely following ISO documentation in making the airbags, but I suspect somewhere along the way, the firm had a process failure. While a process failure in the financial industry may not have fatal consequences, it does have serious ones.

Standards exist to drive out failure; in manufacturing, statistical process control occurs when a process is tested repeatedly to ensure a product functions as designed. In managing wealth, you also need a process that has been tested and monitored. Of course, the chance always exists that an adviser will get lucky with investments. But most clients I work with don't want to leave their finances to chance. In my firm, fortunately, they don't have to, because we can control the process.

I learned about the importance of process when I audited service providers to automotive companies. The word *audit* in this case refers to an evaluation of systems, not to an IRS audit. When I performed an audit, it had two parts. Assessing an organization's policies was the first, and whether those policies were being implemented correctly was the second. For example, let's say a manufacturing company outsources the management of its IT infrastructure. When the data leaves the company and goes to the data center, policies exist on how it should be maintained and secured to ensure privacy and prevent corporate espionage. An audit's first step looks at the security policies and such factors as who has access to the building. The second step examines whether the controls are working. This step focuses on tactics and how a company ensures it is accomplishing its objectives. Do you just trust that the people running the data center are doing everything they need to do? No. You investigate how that policy is implemented to understand what could go wrong. Policies are great, but when the rubber meets the road, they have to be designed and operating successfully to accomplish their objectives. If not, the process will eventually fail.

MY VERSION OF ISO

At my firm, we use the term Fiduciary GPS[SM] to describe our process. Just like ISO, we have policies, strategies, and tactics, and we evaluate whether they are implemented as designed. When I created my practice in 2002, I did a great deal of research on how to design a fiduciary process that would best serve my clients. But there was no way to test whether I was accomplishing what I had set out to do. After exploring further, I became aware of the Center for Fiduciary Studies, founded by Trone. The center was working toward promulgating best practices in the financial services industry. An organization evolved called the Centre for Fiduciary Excellence (CEFEX), which accredits investment advisory firms that pass its rigorous testing for adherence to the fiduciary standard. This is an elite group. As of this writing, only 127 firms worldwide possess CEFEX accreditation. In 2007, my firm was one of the first ten in the world to obtain this accreditation, as well as the first to receive it in Michigan, where I'm based. We recently received accreditation for the eleventh year in a row.

I created the Fiduciary GPS^{SM} process not to simply adhere to the fiduciary standard, but to exceed it. I didn't want to focus only on investments and giving the right advice on products. I wanted to offer a holistic approach and ensure that advice considered the impact on taxes and helped clients accomplish their goals. (Holistic in this context refers to how a financial adviser reviews all relevant aspects of a client's financial and life goals, and then considers how they are interrelated.)

FIDUCIARY GPS^{SM} IN ACTION: BRAD AND LYNNE'S STORY

Brad was a successful marketing executive who left his company to start his own manufacturing firm. His boss from his old company was extremely successful financially, so Brad decided to use his adviser, Larry. Brad's former boss made a warm introduction. Brad and his wife, Lynne, had five children; the youngest had special needs. Brad wanted to provide for his family, and he was confident that the adviser was going to do well by him.

After years of working together, Larry left the financial services firm, and Brad was assigned a new adviser. The firm seemed to have a good process in place. They provided tax preparation and advice. They managed investments. But the new adviser completely missed talking to Brad about his child and the importance of wealth transfer. What's more, the products recom-

AMDG Financial's Fiduciary GPS℠ Process

STEP 1: CREATING THE MASTER MAP
We learn about the client's financial situation, goals, and interests.

STEP 2: ORIENTING THE MAP
We present an investment plan and other recommendations based on our analysis of the client's information. We also discuss our approach to investing.

STEP 3: DECISION POINT
The client determines whether to commit to an advisory relationship and accept our recommendations.

STEP 4: INTERIM CHECKPOINT MEETING
A meeting scheduled shortly after the decision point to organize account transfers and other necessary paperwork.

STEP 5: REGULAR CHECKPOINT MEETINGS
We meet at prescribed intervals (usually once or twice a year, depending on the scope of the relationship) to discuss the client's progress toward goals and any changes in the client's situation. Throughout this time, we may also meet with, or seek input from our team of subject-matter experts and/or the client's other advisers. This way, we maintain a holistic view of our client's overall financial picture.

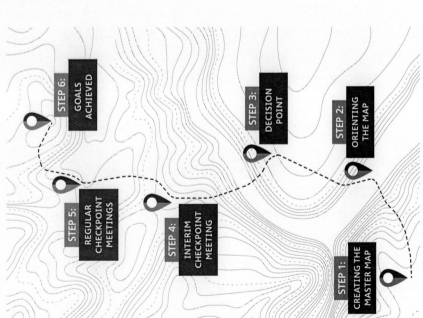

STEP 6: GOALS ACHIEVED

STEP 5: REGULAR CHECKPOINT MEETINGS

STEP 4: INTERIM CHECKPOINT MEETING

STEP 3: DECISION POINT

STEP 2: ORIENTING THE MAP

STEP 1: CREATING THE MASTER MAP

mended to Brad by his adviser now leaned heavily toward variable, variable-index, and fixed annuities, all of which had extremely high fees.

Brad was uncomfortable with the changes, so he began to look for another adviser. He found my firm on the web after doing research into the fiduciary standard. When he came in for the interview, I went through our process with Brad and began to analyze his portfolio. What I found were products with extremely high costs and little or no opportunity to take advantage of future strategic tax strategies. Brad didn't have an exploding airbag when it came to his portfolio; he would likely be OK financially because he and Lynne were consistent savers. But when it came to wealth transfer, he'd have a great deal less left to leave his kids, especially the one with special needs.

My team and I designed a plan for Brad that reduced his costs while increasing the thresholds of money he could save. We implemented a cash balance plan (a deferred shelter for taxable income) that integrated with his 401(k) profit sharing plan. After fifteen years, Brad will have deferred $832,500 in federal tax. That will provide him the opportunity to save more as he gets closer to retirement. At some point, Brad will have to pay taxes on those dollars saved. We designed a twenty- to forty-year strategic cash flow plan with the goal of reducing the amount of tax he'll pay over the long run. He will permanently save

$332,500, money that will grow throughout the lifetime of his special needs child and help support him when Brad and Lynne are gone. Brad's plan went from good to excellent, and I'm proud of the work my team and I did to get it there.

JOHN AND MARY'S STORY

John and Mary, a couple in their midforties, came to me after they had won the lottery. It was an unprecedented experience for them because they had lived a frugal lifestyle for years. John owned a small business and Mary was an art teacher. Throughout their lives, they had scrimped and saved to send their four kids to private religious schools. As a result, up until the lottery windfall, they possessed little in the way of retirement. Now they had the chance to slow down, enjoy their lives with their children and grandchildren, and help provide for the latter's education.

Yet John and Mary were unsure how to navigate providing that help. Hard work was a hallmark of their family. They didn't want their children or grandchildren to ever feel entitled. As part of the Fiduciary GPS℠ process, I spent a significant amount of time with them discussing their views and what the right investment strategy would be to support their goals and objectives. I ended up recommending that the couple work with an estate planning attorney to structure a number of trusts, each with specific objectives. For example, one of the trusts provided for the grandchildren's education, but it was designed so that John and Mary matched their children's contributions. I also helped facilitate conversations with the entire family. As a result, John and Mary were able give to their loved ones in a way that was aligned with their values. Eventually, they built their dream home and are now enjoying a worry-free retirement.

Both these stories illustrate how the Fiduciary GPS℠ process goes far beyond focusing solely on investments. Trone refers to fiduciary standard as the bar. You might want to ask yourself: How far above that bar is my current adviser? Does he or she have a strong process, and am I aware of it? In my view, the process is the solution. It informs strategies and underlying tactics that result in prudent, long-range solutions. It creates efficiency and effectiveness. Strategies and tactics are important, but they must come out of a strong process to avoid short-term problems and the repeated symptoms an unhealthy plan perpetuates. In the next chapter we'll continue to discuss the importance of process, focusing on discovery, communication, and implementation.

PART TWO

STRATEGIC RELATIONSHIP MANAGEMENT

CHAPTER FOUR

PROCESS FOR DISCOVERY

Many financial advisers like to use the analogy of a pilot when describing what they do for clients. They fly the craft, and the client sits comfortably in the cabin. I don't care for that analogy myself because it's primarily about departing from one place and arriving at another, with the client as a passive passenger. There's little discussion about both parties' efforts and intentions, and about how the biggest part of reaching a goal is chunking it down into manageable steps.

I like to compare what I do with my clients to the sport of orienteering, which I participated in as a Cub Scout and Boy Scout leader (eventually passing my love of it down to my son David). In orienteering, you compete with other participants to find your way across an area, usually a countryside, using a map and a compass. (Orienteering can be an individual or team sport.) As a competitor, you get a master map and a punch card at the beginning of the route. At every checkpoint, or control point, you receive a token and your card is punched to prove you showed up. The winner is the one who reaches every control point, in order, with the fastest time.

Embarking on a financial journey is similar to orienteering with a map. When you're navigating an area, you encounter both easy obstacles and challenging ones, terrain that is smooth and difficult. Every participant has unique strengths and weaknesses, and must reach certain markers to ensure a successful journey. Most financial journeys are long-distance endurance races, called "billygoat events" in orienteering. I tend to think of all of my clients' financial plans as billygoat events, and I use orienteering terms for the other types of client meetings we have in our practice as well.

An adviser creates a good relationship with an entrepreneurial client by starting off with a process for discovering what is important to that individual. I liken this process to creating a master map for an orienteering journey. An adviser finds out the terrain of a client's life, his or her goals and objectives, and the obstacles, all the while learning the checkpoints an entrepreneur wants (or needs) to reach or exceed to feel like the journey was successful. One person's control point might be to save

$18,500 a year in her 401(k); another's might be to own a home debt-free by the time he is forty. Every person's race is different.

As the journey unfolds, the map is a guide to assess whether you are on track or need to recalculate. Adviser and client work as a team, like the duos on the TV show *The Amazing Race*. That is why it's so critical to pick an adviser you believe will be an excellent teammate. You want an adviser who understands your checkpoints, because if you miss one—whether it's minimizing your taxes or ensuring wealth protection—you could lose the race.

DISCOVERY AS A COMPATIBILITY TEST

As a financial adviser, I believe the fact-finding or discovery process is key to fulfilling my client's goals. My team and I spend 75 percent of our time up front, trying to understand a client's situation. We spend 15 percent of our time developing recommendations, and the remaining 10 percent goes toward implementing, monitoring, and adjusting a plan. I've found that identifying the right solutions in the first place leads to effective implementation.

Our "master map" meeting includes roughly sixty-five questions. (More information and a checklist on how to prepare for such a meeting can be found in the Appendix.)

Of course we ask financial questions about such issues as retirement needs. But many questions seem unrelated to finance at first glance, such as "What's important to you? What are you trying to accomplish?" I find most people don't want to be a burden on their kids. They want to lead a comfortable lifestyle and provide a legacy—such as contributing to a charity or their grandkids' education, or leaving an inheritance for their children. After the meeting, we analyze and review the information, and make recommendations.

One crucial aspect of the discovery process is that it allows you to observe the adviser "at work" before you make a final decision to sign on. You can see if you two are compatible. It's akin to dating before marriage. Questions to ask yourself about a potential adviser include:

- Is the relationship comfortable? At my firm, my team and I listen deeply. We try to truly understand a situation. If your adviser is more interested in talking than listening, that's a warning sign.
- Is the individual trustworthy? The Financial Industry Regulatory Authority (FINRA) is a nonprofit body authorized by Congress to protect US investors. As I said previously, a financial adviser can hold dual licenses to work as both a broker and an investment adviser. You can check the following sites to find out if clients have filed any ethical violations against a

financial professional for both types of licenses: FIN-RA's BrokerCheck service (https://brokercheck.finra.org) and the US Security and Exchange Commission's Investment Adviser Public Disclosure website (https://adviserinfo.sec.gov/iapd). If you are assessing a fee-only adviser, check to see if they are a member of the National Association of Personal Financial Advisors, located at napfa.org. Every member must sign a fiduciary oath and subscribe to a code of ethics. Finally, the Paladin Registry is a no-cost vetting service that validates and documents adviser qualifications and business practices, matching individual investors to financial fiduciaries. Adviser ratings are available to the public. A five-star rating is the best. A lower rating might indicate conflict-of-interest issues. Meanwhile, some advisers and brokers are licensed as insurance professionals to sell annuity products. To find out about any ethical violations that exist in this arena, check with your individual state's insurance commission.

· Does the adviser have the expertise to know and understand the best ways to take advantage of taxes? Some advisers, even if they are CPAs, are prohibited by their compliance departments from giving tax advice. A failure by a financial adviser to take into account tax burdens and brackets has the potential to severely impact your retirement and the estate you leave for your kids and grandkids.

- Does the adviser care about my needs? You need to assess whether the adviser deeply understands your financial picture within the context of your life and its unique issues.
- Does the adviser look at my situation holistically and provide integrative solutions? Numerous advisers employ a traditional approach, focusing solely on one or two aspects of a client's financial picture. Integrative solutions are synergistic, look at a client's finances as a whole, and integrate tax, financial, and investment management.

Let's look at an example from my practice where I believe clients' needs were addressed with an integrative solution. Entrepreneurs Chris and Jody got married in their late thirties; it was a second marriage for both, and they each had children from their previous marriages. They bought a lake house as a way to help blend the families. Countless happy memories were made within it and on the waterfront, strengthening family relationships. As they approached retirement, they made the decision to sell the property to help fund their lifestyle. This is the point at which Chris and Jody came to us.

The couple felt it was important to pass on their assets to all of their children. However, in our master-map meeting, we found they hadn't discussed any wealth transfer issues with their previous financial adviser. For their situation, we recommended two family trusts, with assets split between spouses. (After we outlined our recommendations, we asked them to review it with their attorney, who confirmed we were on the right track.) Chris's wishes would be followed according to the instructions on his trust, and Jody's on hers. That way, if Chris were to die before Jody—which was statistically likely—there would be no disruption in the family dynamics they had taken such pains to build.

On our advice, Chris and Jody also held a family meeting so everyone could understand the objectives of the estate plan. They explained to the kids that they wanted everyone treated in a thoughtful way. When Chris became ill with lung cancer a decade later and passed away, everyone understood what was being done and why. Jody and her kids remained close to Chris's sons and daughter, instead of becoming more distant (as can often happen). A traditional adviser likely wouldn't have identified the family issue or pursued such an integrative solution. He or she would have focused solely on investments.

THE RELIEF OF TRANSPARENCY

Most people feel incredible stress when discussing finances, because they don't arrive in an adviser's office already understanding everything and knowing how to solve their problems. They don't know it's normal to begin without having all the answers; the master-map process is designed to help clients crystallize their goals and objectives. It can feel uncomfortable at first, but most clients end the first session feeling relieved because their situation is now transparent, perhaps for the first time ever.

John was a hard-driving attorney and entrepreneur who had been managing his own money for years. He came to see us because he thought he might be missing ways to maximize his portfolio. He was initially skeptical of the master-map process because he had expected a conversation centered solely on numbers. Instead, I tried to assess the broader landscape. When I asked him if he and his wife belonged to a faith community and whether that was important to them, he brusquely cut me off.

"Why are you asking such a personal question?" John asked.

I explained that the goal was to identify whether there was future interest in charitable intent for their preferred faith community. If so, we could put that into the master map. Most people, I explained, make gifts from current assets or cash flows. But there might be seeds we could plant to cultivate a future gift that would help reduce taxes or offset the conversion of a traditional IRA to a Roth. I told John about one of our clients who had used a charitable gift to offset a $200,000 conversion.

My response set John back in his chair.

"No other adviser has ever asked that question or shown that level of forethought," he said.

John became a client, and we developed a great relationship built on trust. From the get-go, we demonstrated to him that our master-map process was thoughtful and designed to provide value. A master map is never about the money. It's about what the money can do.

Creating a master map helps people feel more confident, although some are concerned that they're locked into a rigid plan. They're relieved to discover the map isn't static; over time, priorities change, detours happen, and routes need recalculating. Working with a master map and a trustworthy adviser gives you structure and flexibility; it's like having a GPS guiding your path. You need to know where you're going, but if the route changes, you don't have to pull over to find a road map or ask a stranger for directions. Your GPS recalculates and keeps you moving forward.

HITTING CONTROL POINTS

No matter your route, it's wise to build in checkpoints to assess your progress. This happens constantly in orienteering. You look around the terrain and try to identify whether you're in the right place at the right time to get to the next control point. These checkpoints tell you whether you're on pace to finish in time or if you've gotten off track. With a financial plan, meetings serve the same purpose.

One of the questions we ask in our master-map process is how often the client would like to meet. With a new client, we meet frequently—as much as once every other month or once every quarter. Soon, we settle into a cadence. The cadence usually changes when a major life event or stage occurs: a child approaching college age, a job opportunity in another state, retirement, and so forth. In addition to the cadence of each person's life, everyone has a pace particular to them, as in orienteering. Runners with long legs have a different pace than those with short ones.

Frequent meetings can be useful, but be wary if an adviser has a blanket rule of meeting quarterly. Often these pre-scribed meetings are nothing more than performance reports or recaps of market activity. Find out exactly what the meeting will entail.

An entrepreneur's life is busy, and even with a strong relationship with a financial adviser, checkpoint meetings can become a low priority, taking time away from family and business. But they are essential to keep you oriented to your master map. Your adviser must be made aware of any new obstacles or information so he or she can help guide you. Our client Brittany, for example, had a son, Jake, who had initially planned to join the Peace Corps. He backed out and decided to go to a four-year college. Brittany planned to automatically pay for her son's college tuition out of the cash flow from her business. Fortunately, she mentioned Jake's change of heart to us. We explained to Brittany that she would be paying the tuition with after-tax dollars. She was in the highest tax bracket, 39 percent. Coupled with state tax, she would be paying 43 percent in taxes on that money. A loan was a better option for Jake's tuition. She could instead pay 7 percent interest on the minimum payments and shelter the rest of the money in a retirement plan, allowing it to grow, tax-deferred. Brittany went with our recommendation.

Another client, Bruce, told us at a checkpoint meeting that he had decided to put an apartment building he owned up for sale. He wanted to bank the money for retirement. We counseled Bruce to do a 1031 exchange instead, a tax strategy that would enable him to avoid being taxed at 23.8 percent in capital gains. With an exchange, Bruce was able to buy another piece of property in the state where he planned to retire, deferring capital gains. He plans to move into the new property in retirement; at that time, he may have the opportunity to reduce the tax impact of the gains.

Both Brittany and Bruce were able to maximize their

portfolio and minimize taxes because we had excellent communication. In the next chapter we'll focus more on what a strong process for communication looks like between financial adviser and client.

CHAPTER FIVE

PROCESS FOR COMMUNICATION

When I read surgeon Atul Gawande's description of the three types of doctors in his second book, *Being Mortal*, I realized financial advisers could be categorized the same way. Gawande writes:

- The paternalistic doctor tells patients what to do.
- The informative doctor sits down with you and goes through all of the different options you have regarding your particular health issue. However, the reasons why one option might be better than another are not fully explained. He or she doesn't assist you when it comes to making decisions.
- The interpretive doctor gives you information and helps you understand and focus on making the best

decision for yourself. They are on the journey with you.

With financial advisers, some are paternalistic, telling you their strategies and insisting you should follow them. Others are informative, but they fail to help you fully understand the strategies they implement. An interpretive adviser takes you through a process that educates you on *all* your options. He or she helps you sift through the incessant, confusing noise of the market and the media with the goal of serving you and your family. In my view, an interpretive adviser provides the most value.

Finding the right interpretive adviser depends in part on the intention and expectation you bring to your search and into your discovery meeting. If you walk into a meeting and say, "Hey, make me money!" an interpretive adviser will have a very different response than that of a paternalistic or even an informative one. The interpretive adviser is going to ask numerous questions, including: Why do you want to make money? What's important about money to you? What are your goals and objectives?

TAILORED COMMUNICATION

A successful relationship with an interpretive adviser is carried out via a process involving strong relationship management and communication. In my practice, for example, we use a CRM system. We automate reminders and communication, but they are not impersonal. They are tailored to each client, linked to the client's master map, and clear on times, agendas, and content for upcoming meetings. Nothing is left to chance.

The way a trustworthy, interpretive adviser works may be counterintuitive to the way an entrepreneur does. An entrepreneur may let his or her schedule slide—I often say that if scheduling a meeting is left to an entrepreneur, it may never get on the calendar. An interpretive adviser won't let that happen. He or she understands the importance of communication and knows you need to talk about how your goals are evolving over time; the journey is a collaborative one.

Entrepreneurs should welcome this partner into their process, because an interpretive adviser offers a complementary skillset. In his book *Traction*, entrepreneur Gino Wickman talks about the value of the unique relationship between entrepreneurs, who are visionaries, and "integrators." An integrator manages many of the day-to-day operations, leaving the visionary to do what he or she does best. When it comes to your financial life, think of yourself as the visionary, and the interpretive adviser as your integrator. The integrator builds bridges between your personal and business lives. Communicate with them often.

A FOUR-STAGE COMMUNICATION PROCESS

For optimal communication, I use a process that establishes the responsibilities of the adviser and entrepreneur. It has four stages.

Iterative Communication Process Between Adviser and Client

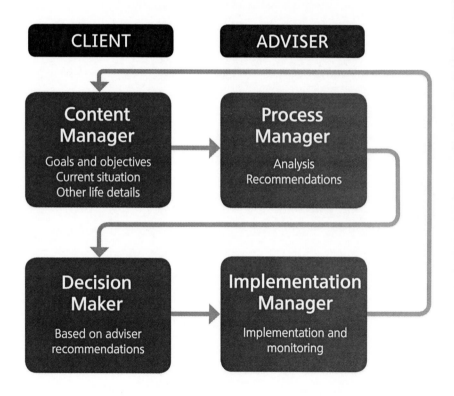

1. The first responsibility of the entrepreneur is to be the content manager. This means knowing the "here and now," the goals and objectives, and anything else that

comprises the terrain of his or her life. The entrepreneur is responsible for sharing that information with the financial adviser, even information that on the surface doesn't seem relevant.

2. The interpretive adviser takes this content, puts it through a robust process, and comes up with alternative solutions. He or she presents the solutions and assists the entrepreneur in understanding them, recommending an approach based on what best accomplishes the entrepreneur's goals and objectives.

3. The entrepreneur makes a decision based on the solutions and recommendations provided by the adviser.

4. The adviser implements the entrepreneur's decision and monitors it until the client provides new content. At this point, that feedback kicks off another round of analysis and further communication, implementation, and monitoring.

Responsibility for this communication process is iterative and ongoing. Let's look at the communication process in the context of Ken and Joy's situation. Ken is a tech entrepreneur, and Joy works at a corporate job. They have one child, and Joy wants to quit work to have another. But both of them are worried that Joy leaving her job will reduce their opportunity to retire early. In stage one, the couple shares the information with their interpretive financial adviser, Gina. In stage two, Gina develops options and presents them. One option is for Ken to consider saving more outside his 401(k) plan. Another is for the couple to put off buying a new home for another three years. A third is for Ken to hire Joy part time after her maternity leave ends and for Joy to start contributing to a separate 401(k) plan.

In stage three, Ken and Joy decide to go with the third option of having Joy work at Ken's company part time after the baby is born and contribute to her own 401(k) plan. The part-time income and tax-deferred savings will keep them on track for retirement. In stage four, Gina plans to monitor the couple's finances for the three years after the baby is born until they are ready to buy a new house. Any new information from Ken and Joy, or any changes in their financial or investment position communicated from Gina, will cause the process to iterate or start over.

WALLY'S STORY

Structured communication processes like these are often crucial in an entrepreneurial business, where cash flow often fluctuates wildly from year to year. Wally, for example, is a Cleveland-based tech entrepreneur and self-professed computer nerd who designed a financial organization app for young families. He is thirty-two and married, with a toddler.

In stage one, Wally shares content with his adviser: his

app is taking off, and he and his wife, Susie, are on track to make $232,000 this year. One of his goals is to discuss how to reduce his tax burden. Another is how to plan ahead for retirement. Based on the post-reform 2018 tax rules, Wally will be in the 24 percent marginal tax bracket when his taxable income hits the $165,000 mark. This is the first time Wally has ever had this level of income, and he hasn't been able to save much until now. He wants to ensure he and his wife, Susie, will retire well. It took Wally two years to design the app. He knows that the following year, as he works on a new app, his income won't be as high. Meanwhile, Wally also has a commitment to give a significant amount of his income to charity.

In stage two, Wally's financial adviser analyzes the information, develops options, and presents them. One plan particularly appeals to Wally: he and Susie would contribute $18,500 each to a 401(k) as well as create a donor-advised fund, a philanthropic vehicle. The fund allows donors to make a charitable contribution and receive immediate tax benefits. Wally decides to create one and give $30,001 to it this year (the action marks stage three in the communication process). Wally doesn't have to decide immediately which worthy causes to support with the fund, but contributing to it now lets him take the deduction. Later, he can determine which charities will receive the money. Combined with the 401(k) contributions, Wally and Susie's taxable income is now below $165,000, the cutoff for the 22 percent tax bracket.

In stage four, Wally's adviser makes a three-year plan around the tax issues and the donor-advised fund. In the short term, the adviser will monitor that Wally's income will indeed be down in 2019 and maintain the plan of continuing the retirement contributions so the couple can stay in the lower tax bracket. In 2020, if a new app takes off, the adviser will see that Wally contributes to the donor-advised fund again, simultaneously keeping him in that lower bracket and allowing him to keep to his commitment to support charitable causes. The adviser will also explore other tax-advantaged options for the couple to save even more for retirement.

Wally comes from a typical hardworking Midwest Rust Belt household. He doesn't want to wind up twenty years down the road being in the same place financially that he was in when he started his career, which is what happened with his folks. For the long term, the adviser creates a ten- to twenty-year plan addressing both taxes and advanced planning. To implement it, Wally commits to meeting every month from September through December in the current year. Wally also commits to a spring review meeting to see if changes are needed.

CREATING STRONG STRUCTURES

Wally felt relieved and much less stressed with the dual planning. His worries about the future were assuaged. A strong communication process gives you confidence because you know whether or not you're on track. Baseball player Mickey Mantle used to say, "If you don't know where you're going, you might not ever get there." Creating wealth comes down to crystallizing your objectives. Crystal structures change all the time, but as they build on each other, they get stronger. In a well-laid process, you get all the pieces in place so, eventually, your plan grows strong enough to support your journey. Checkpoint meetings test your plan's strength and ensure you're moving in the right direction.

CHAPTER SIX

PROCESS FOR IMPLEMENTATION

No process can succeed without an ethical framework to support it. I learned this lesson when I was twenty-three and working as the general manager for a Volkswagen dealership my father owned on the west coast of Florida. One morning I received a call from a supplier. They wanted a $500 payment for a batch of lifetime fluorescent light bulbs we had ordered. Except we hadn't ordered them. I'd never seen a purchase order or an invoice.

I called the parts manager to ask him about the invoice. He told me he didn't know anything about it either. The supplier had provided me with the purchase order number, so I asked the parts manager to bring me the purchase-order book, in case he had forgotten about it.

But the order wasn't in the book. When the parts manager left for the evening, I went back to his department to look for the order, thinking it may have gotten lost and was somewhere on his desk. I found it balled up in the bottom of his trash can.

My dad had acquired the business six months earlier, and all we knew about the parts manager was that he was in his midfifties and had worked at our location for fifteen years. He had been in the business for over three decades. He seemed to be a hard worker who enjoyed time with his family and liked to boat and fish. The day after I found the purchase order in his trash can, I called him into my office to ask him about it. He said he wasn't sure why he threw it away or lied about it. Something smelled fishy, and I terminated him, which wasn't easy because he was the first employee I had ever fired, and he was twice my age. I took over the position, and a few weeks later, I got a call from another vendor asking me if I wanted the same deal he'd had with the former parts manager: receiving kickbacks, like guns and fly rods in exchange for doing business exclusively with him.

I realized that this was a failure of process. When my dad and I took over, we had assumed the vendor relationships in place were appropriate. We didn't have a process to evaluate those relationships or to obtain competitive quotes. The parts manager was making all of the decisions without any checks and balances. This was a formative experience. It clued me in to the importance of having controls in place to successfully implement and manage a process. The lesson came home to me again years later when Volkswagen hit the news for cheating on diesel emissions tests to meet environmental standards. I found it particularly painful because I had admired the company for years and have owned quite a few Volkswagens. With the parts manager and with Volkswagen itself, a failure of process, leadership, and integrity occurred.

THE IMPORTANCE OF BEHAVIORAL GOVERNANCE

The inspiration for my work, as I discussed in Chapter 2, is financial leader Don Trone. Over the years, the Nobel Foundation has awarded many prizes for work in economics and finance. Past awards focused on primarily the mathematical approach to economics and finance. In 2017, Richard Thaler received the Nobel Prize for his work in behavioral economics, which includes the subfield of behavioral finance, the study of the emotional reasons people make their financial decisions. Trone and his colleagues at 3ethos believe that investment success is largely determined by the appropriate application of behavioral finance and behavioral governance. With behavioral finance, the lens is on the behavior of the individual investor. With behavioral

governance, the focus is on the leadership, stewardship, and governance of the financial adviser, trustee,
or investment committee.

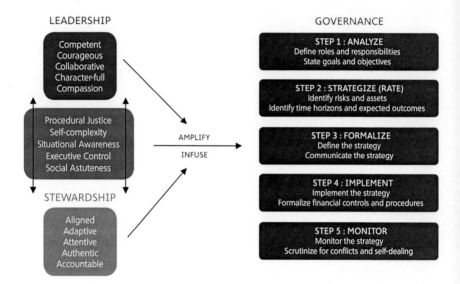

It's critical for you to understand the process behind the
adviser or firm with whom you're considering working
because a successful outcome is dependent upon leadership and stewardship. Trone and his colleagues have
developed a leadership movement named L5, of which I
am a part. The movement and its name were inspired by
author Jim Collins's essays describing a Level 5 leader in
his book *Good to Great*. For Trone, an L5 designation is for
exemplary financial professionals and indicates that they
use particular training, underlying tools, and the behavioral governance framework in the execution of their

processes. An L5 professional employs procedural justice, vision and inspiration, self-complexity, situational awareness, executive control, and social astuteness. How well they perform is tied to their level of conscientiousness.

FIDUCIARY ACCOUNTABILITY

By this point in the book, you know the fiduciary standard refers to an adviser being loyal to a client's best interests from an investment perspective. When choosing an adviser, it's important to determine whether he or she is a fiduciary in more than name alone. For even when legislation exists to enforce a standard, some advisers try to work around it.

To recap from Chapter 2, let's say Adviser A and Adviser B both present themselves as fiduciaries and both receive commissions. But Adviser A receives commissions without disclosing to the client when he switches hats from fee-based adviser to broker. Adviser B receives commissions but, as a fiduciary, only at a percentage that he and the client agreed upon in the beginning of the relationship. Both brokers are fiduciaries when they give advice, but only one, Adviser B, is when selecting products.

How can you know if you're heading in the right direction with an adviser? First, determine whether he or she is adheres to the following best practice model:

PERIODIC TABLE
of GLOBAL FIDUCIARY PRACTICES
for INVESTMENT ADVISERS

PRACTICE 1.1

The Investment Adviser demonstrates an awareness of fiduciary duties and responsibilities.

PRACTICE 2.1

An investment time horizon has been identified for each investment objective of the client.

PRACTICE 2.2

An appropriate risk level has been identified for each client.

PRACTICE 1.2

Investments and investment services provided are consistent with applicable governing documents.

PRACTICE 1.3

The roles and responsibilities of all involved parties (fiduciaries and non-fiduciaries) are defined and documented.

PRACTICE 2.3

An expected return to meet each investment objective has been identified.

PRACTICE 2.4

Selected asset classes are consistent with the client's time horizon and risk and return objectives.

PRACTICE 1.4

The Investment Adviser identifies conflicts of interest and addresses conflicts in a manner consistent with the duty of loyalty.

PRACTICE 1.5

Agreements, including service provider agreements under the supervision of the Investment Adviser, are in writing and do not contain provisions that conflict with fiduciary standards of care.

PRACTICE 2.5

Selected asset classes are consistent with implementation and monitoring constraints.

PRACTICE 2.6

The investment policy statement contains sufficient detail to define, implement, and monitor the client's investment strategy.

PRACTICE 1.6

Client assets are protected from theft and embezzlement.

PRACTICE 2.7

When socially responsible investment strategies are ejected, the strategies are structured appropriately.

PRACTICE 4.1

Periodic reports compare investment performance against appropriate index, peer group, and investment policy statement objectives.

PRACTICE 3.1

A reasonable due diligence process is followed to select each service provider in a manner consistent with obligations of care.

PRACTICE 4.2

Periodic reviews are made of qualitative and/or organizational changes of Investment Managers, and other service providers.

PRACTICE 4.3

Control procedures are in place to periodically review policies for trading practices and proxy voting.

PRACTICE 3.2

When statutory or regulatory investment safe harbors are elected, each client's investment strategy is implemented in compliance with applicable provisions.

PRACTICE 3.3

Decisions regarding investment strategies and types of investments are documented and made in accordance with fiduciary obligations of care.

PRACTICE 4.4

Periodic reviews are conducted to ensure that investment-related fees, compensation, and expenses are fair and reasonable for the services provided.

PRACTICE 4.5

There is a process to periodically review the organization's effectiveness in meeting its fiduciary responsibilities.

Second, find out if a process exists for the work ahead, whether it is monitored, and if the adviser takes a team approach.

Finally, look for evidence that they have a good governance system in place.

THE EVOLUTION OF A FIDUCIARY QUALITY MANAGEMENT SYSTEM

When I was first designing business processes for my new firm, I was inspired by one of Trone's first books, *Procedural Prudence for Fiduciaries*. The American Institute of CPAs recommended it for CPAs who acted in a fiduciary capacity. (Soon after publishing the book, Trone created the Center for Fiduciary Studies. The center morphed into an organization called Fi360, which still exists today. The body of knowledge that Trone and his colleagues used to create best practices for investment advisers is now a global standard used by CEFEX in its examinations of investment advisers around the world.)

Procedural Prudence for Fiduciaries was a watershed book for me. I knew I wanted to be the best adviser possible for my clients. I knew a fee-only investment advisory practice grounded in the fiduciary standard was the way to go. But I also realized I didn't have all the answers on how to do that, and I needed my company's work independently evaluated against a standard of best practices. As a result of an evaluation, I could implement recommendations and improve. Since 2007, my firm has gone through the annual accreditation process from CEFEX. To see our accreditation certificate, go to: https://tinyurl.com/amdg-cefex. CEFEX updates the standards every year, which forces me to push myself to provide the best services possible. It's worth restating that having a process and documenting it is admirable, but operating it efficiently and effectively is another thing altogether.

The accreditation process is rigorous and involves an examination. For example, the first high-level best practice is for an investment adviser to demonstrate an awareness of fiduciary duties and responsibilities. The criteria for that practice are for the adviser to comply with all fiduciary laws and rules that apply to adviser services; to comply with all applicable practices and procedures in a prudent practices handbook; and to adhere to professional standards of conduct and codes of ethics required by law, regulations, their firm, and all applicable organizations of which they are a member.

Another requirement is for the firm's investment products and investment services to be consistent with applicable governing documents. You must be, for example, in compliance with laws around the Employee Retirement Income Security Act (ERISA), the Investment Advisers

Act of 1940 and its underlying regulations, the Uniform Prudent Investor Act (UPIA), the Uniform Prudent Management of Institutional Funds Act (UPMIFA), and the Uniform Management of Public Employee Retirement Systems Act (UPERSA). Different laws require you to do certain things when serving in particular capacities—for example, ERISA might require a certain type of fiduciary file because of the types of plans you're serving.

A rigorous accreditation process such as the one from CEFEX is, in essence, an investment fiduciary quality management system, one that requires an adviser to meet high ethical standards. It is a piece of the pie, but it is not the whole pie. Looking back at the Volkswagen emissions scandal, it's clear behavioral governance was lacking. Volkswagen suffered a failure of leadership. From a stewardship perspective, the principles of the organization weren't aligned with the long-term objectives of being competitive in the marketplace in fifty years. Amazingly, they hadn't considered the impact if the cheating was discovered. Leadership looked only at profits.

In his book *Leader Metrics*, Trone writes, "We witness a person's competence by their achievements and capabilities, but a person's true character remains below the surface until it's revealed through their behavior." You can evaluate an adviser's character by, for example, finding out whether they are involved in their community in positions requiring trust or leadership. Do your due diligence.

You're looking for solid processes, but that doesn't mean your relationship with your adviser will be cold and unfeeling. Advisers can implement processes and remain compassionate. Ask yourself: Can they put themselves in your shoes? Do they understand you, or are they just paying lip service? Identifying compassion is a soft skill, and some of us are better at soft skills than others. Sometimes, gut feelings get overridden by appearances. Don't be seduced by a flashy financial adviser driving a Jaguar with vanity plates.

In other words, don't be like Juliet, a client who failed to follow her gut with her initial choice of adviser. She went to him for years without feeling like she was getting anywhere. Every time she sat down with him, he moved her from one annuity product to another. There was no comprehensive strategy, no master plan or process behind his recommendations and decisions.

Juliet came to us with her portfolio. We analyzed it and discussed many of the issues we saw, including the high fees and commissions she had paid for the annuity products. When we learned who her adviser was, we also discussed the red flags apparent on his website. There were no endorsements, because that's not permissible in the financial services industry, but there was a great deal of slick puffery that made the adviser appear to be a leader in the industry when he was not. All he does is sell financial products and reap large commissions. Juliet had not spent enough time getting to know her adviser, and he had no process for a client to do so. If she had looked behind the curtain, like Dorothy did in *The Wizard of Oz*, she would have seen the flashy broker was not an all-knowing authority.

When people first come to see me, I make it clear our master-map creation process is thorough. There's cost in time, I say, but not in dollars. In the last of our three-meeting series, we have our decision-point meeting. During that meeting, we answer all a client's questions and outline the next steps, should we commit to moving forward. That meeting is the basis upon which we launch any relationship, proceeding with efficiency, trust, and clear expectations. Once the foundation is set, it's much easier to address strategic wealth management with practical strategies, the focus of Part 3.

PART THREE

STRATEGIC WEALTH MANAGEMENT

CHAPTER SEVEN

INVESTMENT CONSULTING

The business of financial advising has evolved, much like the automobile industry has where I live, just outside Detroit. I'm fascinated by how cars have become some of the most complex products we use on a daily basis. From the engine and the emissions system to the transmission and the climate control system—there's nothing simple about cars today. They are highly engineered. They are so complicated that few backyard mechanics exist anymore.

Think of the process that took us from the Ford Model T to the electric Chevrolet Volt. The Model T had a naturally aspirated carburetor on an engine with a manual transmission; you had to change the gears yourself if you wanted to go anywhere. Then the auto industry started turning out cars with fuel injection and computer controlled systems that notify mechanics when something is off. Batteries came along next in our quest for a more efficient use of power and energy. Now, cars like the Chevrolet Volt have a combination of batteries and small onboard gas powered generators for electricity (as well as additional systems that re-generate electricity through braking or other gearing). When I drive my Volt, I am amazed how seamlessly the generator kicks on and off in order to stabilize the battery temperature depending on the weather.

The Model T averaged between thirteen and twenty-one miles per gallon; fuel-injected vehicles stretched efficiency from fifteen to forty-five. The Chevy Volt can go between forty-two and over 250 miles per gallon. The more engineers learned, the more sophisticated cars became.

You and I could never create cars with the complexity of a Volt. We rely on engineers who work together to design the vehicle's highly cooperative and interdependent systems. In a similar way, today's quality wealth management processes include far more than investment consulting. True wealth management requires deep expertise and a high level of skillful monitoring.

The financial services industry has evolved in much the same way, moving from basic investment consulting to the sophisticated systems I've outlined in the previous chapters. Yet not every financial adviser has evolved as quickly. Many operate like an old carburetor, offering only cookie-cutter plans. These advisers aren't efficient, and the costs for the mileage you receive for their services are expensive. But advisers implementing ISO-like standards and management operate like a Volt. They look for twenty-first century strategies with optimal efficiency. They tightly integrate their investment process to minimize taxes. They monitor legal mechanisms to control the transfer of wealth to heirs and ensure clients have the right levels of insurance—all of which increases opportunity to support charitable gifting strategies (which we will discuss in Chapter 11). These advisers execute intentional wealth management. But for the most part, they are the exception rather than the rule in my industry. They are the Volts, the leading-edge doers demonstrating where the field is going.

RAJ'S STORY: HIGH RETURNS, HIGH TAXES

A twenty-first century financial adviser creates a vision for the future that accommodates the short-term view and the long-term one. Unfortunately, many advisers still think only about the short term and how much they can profit from clients.

Let's look at what happened with a client named Raj, a tool-and-die manufacturer with a midsized company in

Detroit. Raj came to me solely to have his tax return prepared. He already had a financial adviser. When Raj and his wife, Rena, returned to my office to discuss and sign their return, I reluctantly had to inform them they owed $130,000 in federal income tax.

Needless to say, the couple was unhappily surprised. I explained that Raj's adviser had been extremely active in managing his portfolio, buying and selling tech stocks like Facebook, Apple, and Google (and making a lot of money in commissions). On the surface it looked to Raj like he was having significant gains in his portfolio, but in reality, the taxes were killing him. All his capital gains were short term, meaning they were taxed as ordinary income because he had held them less than a year. If Raj had held them longer, he would have been taxed at lower rate. In addition, other short-term investments didn't stay in Raj's portfolio long enough to be treated as qualified dividend income, which also caused the dividends to be taxed at a higher rate. It was a double whammy. (For more information on capital gains and dividends, see the Appendix.)

Raj's adviser had not implemented an allocation strategy to increase tax efficiency. Such a strategy ensures you pay less tax because of how you allocate across different account types. Raj's adviser had done what many advisers do, which is have clients hold exactly the same allocation in an IRA as they hold in a taxable account. That's inefficient, but advisers go that route because it takes them out of harm's way legally; they won't be held responsible for making tax decisions for their clients. There's a more efficient way, and that's to understand the nature of the investment, how the income from it is taxed, and where best to put that income. If Raj's broker had been trading stocks within his IRA or his Roth IRA, Raj would not have been immediately hit so hard. Meanwhile, Raj's corporate bonds from companies Ford and Delphi were in a taxable account; they should have been placed inside his traditional IRA to shelter them from being taxed as ordinary income. Yet Raj's municipal bonds were in that IRA, an illogical place as well, since they are exempt from federal tax and don't need sheltering.

Raj's allocation made little sense. Every client's situation and tax bracket are different, of course, yet the main point an adviser should be discussing with you is not returns, but returns after taxes. Different investments carry different tax implications. Again, a twenty-first century financial adviser whose business is highly engineered operates like that Volt. He or she looks at every aspect of your financial picture.

LOOK FOR A STRATEGIC ADVISER

Active managers and advisers who constantly buy and sell

stocks or mutual funds, like Raj's adviser did, are often seen as master builders who have all the answers. That's an old-school method, as is the more passive strategy of buy and hold. Today's world requires something different: *strategic* management. I firmly believe that, overall, a client's financial picture should be highly engineered and strategically managed.

My team and I gather information from the client and put it through our process, which informs a long-term strategy, including the development and implementation of an allocation. We then look for mutual fund managers whose funds will implement the strategy. The goal is to find low-cost institutional funds that have low turnover and high tax efficiency, and maintain their asset class. You don't need to buy individual stocks; you're better off diversifying your risk with mutual funds.

I use the analogy of LEGO toys to explain the strategy. When you rip open the LEGO box and dump the bricks out onto the table, what also falls out is a little white piece of paper, the instructions. If you snap the pieces together in a particular way, it delivers the model pictured. Now imagine that those LEGO pieces represent individual mutual funds. If you snap together a financial portfolio model, but a year from now every individual manager changes the size, color, and shape of their blocks, will your model look anything like it did when you snapped it together? No. Each block represents how my team and I are trying to expose the portfolio to that asset class. We look for managers who are consistent in their size, color, and shape, so that we can snap together an efficient, effective strategy.

Having a strategy doesn't mean the details of your "model" never change, because they can and often do. Imagine that each block in your model is made of a sponge material, and notice how it reacts to humidity changes that represent the ups and downs of the stock market. Depending upon the humidity of the marketplace, the LEGO model (your portfolio) shrinks or grows. One sponge will have more moisture in it than the other, and little cracks and spaces will appear between the bricks. When that happens, the moisture is squeezed out of one block and put it into another. That shift suggests we need to rebalance your portfolio, which means buying or selling assets to maintain your allocation strategy. With rebalancing, we adjust the model, not to change size, shape, or style, but to refit the pieces together, maintaining diversification across twelve thousand to fifteen thousand underlying company stocks worldwide. The strategy is tax efficient and effective while balancing asset class exposure. That's true diversification. Let's take Raj's example and apply this approach. (Please keep in mind this is a complex arena requiring a skilled adviser.) If he had gone through a process such as ours, he would have been diversified across far more asset classes. We would have set things up differently to minimize tax implications and improve tax efficiency over the long term. Raj held mostly large US companies in the S&P 500; we would have traded only when his portfolio needed rebalancing. In addition, we would have allocated his holdings across his account types differently: joint accounts would go under the taxable category; the IRA and 401(k) accounts under tax deferred; and the Roth IRA accounts under nontaxable. Such a strategy considers the income generated by the underlying holdings. It strategically moves both capital gain and municipal bond assets to taxable accounts. It moves ordinary income assets to his retirement accounts. His allocation would shift over time, but without the daily trading and resulting tax impacts that he experienced with his financial adviser.

CHAPTER EIGHT

WEALTH ENHANCEMENT

As your investment strategy evolves and your wealth grows, you enter an even more complex realm: wealth enhancement and advanced planning. At this stage, planning should be about more than an investment strategy.

If you're like many entrepreneurs, you separate your work life and personal life when it comes to creating wealth. You hand your money over to a broker or adviser to invest it, not thinking about how the money has been pulled out of your business and taxed, and is now worth 30 to 40 percent less than before you took it out. What if you thought more broadly about how your resources could be used? Instead of compartmentalizing your finances, for example, consider what opportunities exist to invest through a pretax retirement plan to shelter that money and leverage it now while you are in a high tax bracket. Then you would take it out in the future at a lower tax rate.

Integration makes sense, but too often, when entrepreneurs leave their corporate jobs to strike out on their own, they take an "employee mentality" with them as far as finances. They do what they've always done. Returning to the analogy of the Ford Model T and the Chevy Volt, sometimes entrepreneurs are focused on an outdated design, and they can't see the possibility of a beautiful integration of systems.

Successful wealth enhancement is about being proactive. It's about giving increased consideration to federal, state, and payroll taxes all the time, not just at the end of the year (or quarter). It's about knowing how to use retirement accounts (in concert with how much you earn). As a business owner you have the opportunity to do things like design and implement your own 401(k) and determine whether or not you want to match employee contributions and/or have profit sharing.

Remember Edie, from Chapter 1? She left her job as a high-powered management consultant to start a company specializing in CRM systems for small businesses in the Detroit area. Her new company was doing great, but Edie wasn't equipped to navigate the financial side of being an entrepreneur. She had no idea that as a leader of a company and a contributor to her family, she could use both roles to increase her wealth.

For example, Edie was still using her longtime CPA adviser, Beth, for her return, and Beth was slow to plan ahead regarding recent tax law changes. A change in marginal tax rates lowered the rate in Edie's bracket. She had no idea she was able to receive what is called a Section 199A Qualified Business Income Deduction. Payments to contractors could not be included in the deduction. But Beth didn't talk to Edie about considering hiring a number of her contractors as employees in order to take advantage of 199A. As a result, Edie still thought contractors were the cheapest way to go.

SHELTERING INCOME VIA AN ENHANCED PLAN

Edie knew saving was important. When she started her business, she did implement a 401(k) plan with a payroll company. The process was easy, and it was up and running immediately. But it was a cookie-cutter plan. It didn't address Edie's objectives to the highest level possible and Beth was no help in exploring the ins and outs of this solution.

Successful entrepreneurs are paid well. They have a high W-2 wage and high distributions, and they pay a significant amount of taxes. But again, entrepreneurs like Edie often do what they did when they worked for someone else—get paid and then use a 401(k) to shelter $18,500 (which is the upper limit for those under age fifty, after which it goes to $24,500). If, as an entrepreneur, you take a step back and ask how you can take a long-term view to enhance your wealth, you can design a plan to shelter more income from high levels of taxation. If Edie had worked through her goals and objectives with the right adviser, she could have increased the opportunity to shelter income through an additional profit sharing feature in her 401(k) plan or implemented an additional cash balance plan. A cash balance plan is a pension plan, but it is not the traditional kind. Countless business owners are wary of pension plans because of a preconceived idea that many companies fail because they can't meet pension plan obligations. However, a combination of a cash balance plan and a 401(k) plan allows entrepreneurs to save more of their own money (up to 95 percent of total contributions) if implemented correctly.

This year, Edie is on track to have a W-2 income of $500,000. In a traditional plan, she could shelter $24,500 in her 401(k) because she is over fifty. However, that doesn't take her W-2 income down too far. But if she adds in the profit sharing plan and the cash balance one, putting another $24,500 in the former and $250,000 in the latter, now she has a W-2 income of $200,000. If she and her family don't need that money to live on daily; why pay 35 percent, the second-highest marginal tax bracket, plus state income tax (4.25 percent) and payroll taxes (1.2 percent)? With the new strategy, Edie reaps a tax savings in 2018 of about $100,000. Meanwhile, when she hits retirement, she will likely be in a lower tax bracket, stretching her savings even further.

RETIREMENT PLANS AND A LONG-TERM TAX FLOW STRATEGY

To maximize savings, you must also understand how to use the different types of retirement accounts. For example, let's say Edie's husband, Frank, decides to leave his job to be a stay-at-home dad with their two girls as they enter junior high. Edie's income puts them above the limit to take a deductible IRA contribution for Frank, and it also prohibits him from making a Roth IRA contribution. But he can make a nondeductible IRA contribution and immediately roll it into a Roth IRA. Frank can continue to build his savings in the Roth account through these yearly "back-door" contributions. (For more information, see the Appendix.) The contributions are taxed upfront, but the growth and withdrawals are not, setting the family up to enhance their wealth in the future. Such a strategy is highly complex, which is why you need an adviser who knows how to navigate this arena.

Another important strategy for entrepreneurs is to work

with an adviser who will create a twenty- to forty-year cash flow tax plan. If Edie shelters the money in the strategies we just discussed, she'll do so for about twenty years until it's time to retire. However, at that time, Edie will have to take required minimum distributions from her retirement accounts. She'll potentially turn on Social Security. She may have other sources of income by that time. While Edie will likely be in a lower tax bracket in retirement, it's still imperative to take such factors into account and design a strategic plan to ensure she supports her lifestyle and minimizes her taxes.

EMPLOYEE BENEFITS

Employee benefits are another focus point for wealth enhancement. As we've discussed, strategies such as a profit-sharing plan increase the amount you can save. So do two additional benefits: flexible spending accounts and health savings accounts (FSAs and HSAs). These work like savings accounts for qualifying medical expenses. Employees contribute pretax, reducing their tax liability. Funds can be used for deductibles or copays and for qualifying prescriptions and medical equipment. (An FSA allows income to be deferred for childcare.) FSAs and HSAs have a number of differences, including how they are structured and the contribution limits. Both allow you and your employees to shelter income while you're in the highest-earning tax brackets. HSA balances may accumulate and be invested for growth and use in the future, while FSAs are "use it or lose it" pretax accounts. When using an FSA with an HSA, it is called a limited FSA and has special limitations to comply with IRS rules. Not all HSA plans are the same, and in fact, some are expensive. Working with an adviser who can point out these differences and efficiently guide you, and even possibly manage your HSA account options, is another way to effectively use your adviser to your advantage. Meanwhile, you may have heard of health reimbursement accounts, or HRAs. HRAs are for employer contributions only. Employees are reimbursed by the plan after presenting receipts. While they are not a wealth enhancement strategy, entrepreneurs may want to explore them as an employer-based benefit. (For more information on FSAs, HSAs, and HRAs, see the Appendix.)

THE POWER OF A SKILLFUL, TRUSTWORTHY ADVISER

When you're a stressed, overworked entrepreneur such as Edie, it's understandable that you would be tempted by easy, "instant" solutions offered by payroll and insurance companies. Unfortunately, easy doesn't necessarily translate into efficient. It's my belief and experience that you can save more money for yourself and your employees by ensuring you are not in prepackaged retirement plans. The strategies I've described in this chapter are extremely valuable—but they are not simple. To implement them, you need to work with an adviser who knows what he or she is doing. I decided to earn a master's degree in employee benefits law to ensure I could help my entrepreneurial clients take advantage of every opportunity to save and grow wealth. When I work with a client, I not only help design the right plan for them, I help them communicate the benefits of their plan to their employees.

My dad always told me, "You can delegate authority, but you can never delegate responsibility." As a boss, you have a fiduciary duty in choosing plans for employees. A fiduciary adviser has robust processes in place to (1) ensure entrepreneurs meet these duties and (2) reduce or eliminate liability. Selecting and monitoring investments is a significant responsibility that most entrepreneurs believe is alleviated by using their existing adviser. In fact, many advisers may not be responsible for the very thing for which the entrepreneur has engaged them. You don't know what you don't know, and you need someone who does. As my firm's tagline says, "From financial wisdom, better stewardship."

CHAPTER NINE

WEALTH TRANSFER

Even if you've hired the right adviser to make your wealth grow, you are not done managing that wealth. At some point, you will need to think about wealth transfer—making sure your assets go where you want them to go when you die or if you become incapacitated.

Two of my clients recently died of cancer, and their stories illustrate the importance of planning ahead. Gary was a gregarious soul, the type of person everyone likes immediately. Gary left a large marketing company to start a small business selling frozen foods to grocery stores. It had always been his dream to be an entrepreneur. He was a marathon runner and had always felt invincible, yet when he was fifty-two, he was diagnosed with colon cancer. He had ignored warning signs, and by the time he was diagnosed it was too late. The cancer quickly spread to his liver, and Gary passed away within a year.

Gary had no life or disability insurance. He had used the majority of his retirement account funds to start his business, leaving little for himself and his wife, Julia. Still, even as he grew more and more ill, eventually becoming bedridden, Gary remained in denial about advanced planning. When Gary died, he left behind Julia, their twelve-year-old son, and Gary's nineteen-year-old daughter from a previous marriage. Julia was a freelance writer with inconsistent income. After Gary died, she went back to work at a corporate job to bring in a steady paycheck and benefits. To pay off their debt, Julia had to sell the couple's dream home in a beautiful, close-knit community. However, because the home was solely in Gary's name, the title had to go through probate court, delaying Julia's ability to sell it. In addition, she had to hire an attorney to go to court on her behalf. Meanwhile, Gary's son had to change schools and leave his friends. His daughter was forced to transfer to a more affordable university far from her friends and boyfriend. On top of grieving a husband and father, Gary's family had to adjust to a giant loss of stability and social support.

David was the second client who passed away. He was an entrepreneur with a successful real estate development company. David had a blended family of three children.

He, too, was diagnosed with colon cancer around the same time as Gary. However, David had planned years ahead for a crisis. His financial life was extremely complex, yet he had taken the time to work with an adviser and create a solid wealth transfer plan. David owned a business, residential property, and rental properties. He had a large 401(k), IRAs, and other investment accounts. He also had inherited a family farm with oil and gas lease rights. When David received his diagnosis, he had a disability policy and life insurance in place. He had time to oversee revisions to his family trust, and he put the farm into a sub-trust so the income could be used immediately to assist his kids in moving forward. Gary's kids had to navigate adolescence and college with grief and money worries. David's family did not have to deal with asset transfer issues and, while devastated, felt taken care of by him, even in his absence.

WHATEVER YOU DO, DON'T WAIT

If you're like many entrepreneurs, you are intensely focused on your business. You may have a risk-taking personality; maybe you even feel bulletproof. That serves you well when it comes to starting companies and creating innovation. But the shadow side is unpreparedness and the possibility of leaving your family with little understanding of how assets will transfer, exposing them to a great deal of risk. Wealth transfer is about *not* leaving things up to chance if something happens to you or your spouse. It is about putting legal mechanisms in place to ensure your loved ones won't experience chaos and stress on top of grief and loss. Above all, wealth transfer is about being *intentional*.

Most people don't think about wealth transfer and estate planning until they are near retirement. But it doesn't matter if you're thirty-five or sixty-five; you must be prepared, particularly because, as an entrepreneur, your life is more complex than 90 percent of the population. You have complicated legal structures surrounding your business. The company is dependent on you in multiple ways as the pilot of the plane. If you don't leave clear instructions and a strong plan for a copilot, you're setting everyone in your company and your family up for disaster.

I'm aware end-of-life planning isn't a popular, upbeat subject. But when the time arrives, as it does for all of us, you can't underestimate the peace you and your family will experience if your financial affairs are in order. As chair of the Financial Literacy Task Force for the Michigan Association of CPAs (MICPA), I helped create a resource for Hospice of Michigan to help people in this arena. The booklet is called *Financial Affairs at the End of Life*, and it covers everything from prepaid funeral planning to understanding Veterans Affairs benefits, wills, trusts, durable powers of attorney, and more. It's designed to help lucid hospice patients, as well as their families, navigate wealth transfer during what is often a short window of time. For access to MICPA's booklet, visit WayneBTitus3.com/resources.

I also introduced the concept of financial "scrapbooking" to the MICPA. Financial scrapbooking is an exercise where you identify specific risks and ensure you have written instructions in place to address them. For example, a Financial Scrapbook℠ holds items such as your trusts, durable power of attorney, and will. It documents where assets are held, as well as your legal entities and how they operate. If someone needed to operate or wind down your household, it contains important contact information, log-ins, and passwords, household account and subscription information, and more. CPAs across Michigan now use the financial scrapbooking exercise to educate the public on the importance of end-of-life planning. (For more on creating a Financial Scrapbook℠, see the Appendix.)

TRUSTS, WILLS, POWERS OF ATTORNEY, AND SUCCESSION PLANS

If your financial adviser is only concerned with your investment accounts and doesn't understand the legal structure of your business and other interests, you are in trouble. No master map will exist for you and your family when it is most needed. Your financial adviser should understand the legal aspects of wealth transfer, but that doesn't mean he or she needs to be an attorney. Your adviser does need to identify specific wealth transfer issues you might face and help you develop protective solutions. In tandem, the adviser needs a process to address the fast-moving lives most entrepreneurs experience. With an entrepreneur, an idea can quickly turn into a company, which can lead to buying a new building, and so forth, all of which impact a financial picture. In addition, income often fluctuates, arriving from multiple sources. Just as in orienteering, an entrepreneur's master map and terrain constantly change. He or she, with the help of their adviser, must continually take bearings and identify adjustments in the course. Here are the most common aspects of wealth transfer:

TRUSTS AND WILLS

A trust is a legal entity that documents your wealth transfer instructions to your trustee to enforce after your death. (The trustee is the individual you have legally designated to carry out your wishes.) As an entrepreneur, when you leave the office to go on vacation, what's the first thing you do? You sit down with your management team or anyone else who will run things when you're gone, and tell them what to do. Essentially, that is the role of a trust. As they say in law school classes: a trust allows you to reach back from the grave to enforce your fore-most intentions.

One of the biggest differences between a will and a trust is that a will goes through probate court. Probate is the government's legal process for distributing your property. A trust bypasses probate. Many people believe that if you have a will in place, your family won't have to go to probate. That's not true. If your will has assets that need transferring, and those assets have not been arranged to avoid probate, you must go to the probate process. In it, you need a court order to transfer the title of most assets. Your family or loved ones must engage an estate attorney, and that likely won't be cheap. Without a will or a trust, it's left to the government to decide who will distribute your assets as the executor. Probate moves at a snail's pace—usually twelve to eighteen months or more. If your family depends on assets that need transferring, you're putting them in harm's way. Many different kinds of trusts exist—revocable and irrevocable, grantor and nongrantor, and so forth—that is why it is essential to have an adviser who understands the different types of trusts.

COMPLEX FAMILY SITUATIONS

Complex family situations include a second marriage, children from previous marriages, a special needs child, and more. Your wishes can only be directed and accomplished through a trust or multiple trusts. For example, in the case of a special needs child, you can leave a suggestion in a will, document, or letter to your children or spouse, but that doesn't create a legal obligation for them to ensure a special needs child is supported in the way you desire and in a way that won't result in a financial burden to them. Trusts address a myriad of circumstances such as the following:

- An entrepreneur has an eldest child from a prior marriage, and his first spouse is not financially responsible. The entrepreneur creates an irrevocable sub-trust (a trust within a trust) that protects and moves assets designated for that child's benefit upon his death. The former spouse would not have access to it.
- Many times, entrepreneurs make the mistake of making their spouse the beneficiary on everything, but they haven't thought through the "what-ifs" down the road. What if, for example, your spouse remarries, winds up divorcing, and the assets are divvied up, leaving out your kids? A trust with well-considered beneficiary designations ensures assets are protected for your children.
- Addiction is rife across the country. Trusts can include conditions, such as money being held to pay for education only and not to be distributed unless a person remains drug-free for a set period of time.
- Countless relationships have been destroyed over

one sibling being disinherited, at times unintentionally. Siblings or other relatives may sue each other, creating unprecedented stress for entire families. Trusts designate who gets what and can be designed to accommodate family situations that cannot be managed in a will or in the absence of other planning.

DURABLE POWER OF ATTORNEY

A durable power of attorney gives another person the authority to act on your behalf in financial matters if you become incapacitated. Many spouses give each other durable power of attorney for their finances. In contrast, an "ordinary" power of attorney ends when the person who designated it loses the ability to make financial decisions. In either case, these powers of attorney end when you die. At that point, the executor of your estate takes over, although in many cases, the executor may be the same person who held a durable or ordinary power of attorney. (Meanwhile, many parents have durable power of attorney for their college-aged children, for use in the event of an emergency. For more information, see the Appendix.)

SUCCESSION PLANS

Without a succession plan, the value of a business can be decimated upon an entrepreneur's death. When David passed away, he had a strong succession plan in place. His share in his real estate development company was worth $2.1 million. He knew his wife didn't have the background or interest to be engaged or involved, or to take on management decisions after his death. He had arranged for an insurance policy that provided proceeds to the company so it could buy out his wife as a partner.

In contrast, Gary had no succession plan. When he passed away, no one was interested in buying the business because Gary had not made it sustainable. While the accounts had value, he had not planned for a succession buyer. Gary would have been wise to have a plan, one where he, at a minimum, carried an insurance policy that covered his business debt and had conducted an evaluation of the accounts. If he had done so, his wife could have sold it with a business broker as quickly as possible after his death. Gary also could have groomed a successor or identified a competitor or related business as a buyer.

Entrepreneurs tend to be solo fliers. They value independence and freedom. But that also unfortunately creates the freedom to hurt your family. You have to push back against the tendency to rely only on yourself. The ancient Greek philosopher Heraclitus said, "Everything is in a state of flux. Everything flows constantly, and there is nothing permanent except change." Nothing could be truer when it comes to the life of an entrepreneur. You've invested a great deal into your business. You must focus not only on turning it into a financial asset but on ensuring it protects your family if something happens to you.

CHAPTER TEN

WEALTH PROTECTION

As an entrepreneur, you've worked extremely hard and taken many risks to succeed. It's essential you have mechanisms in place to leverage and protect the wealth you've accumulated. Typically, you can accomplish this through insurance, but insurance is complicated and expensive. You must read the fine print. Insurance companies work under what's called the law of large numbers, similar to casinos. Casinos know that when one thousand people walk through the door, 520 of them will lose a significant amount of money, while the remaining 480 might win a little bit. An insurance company's goal is to minimize the cost of those 480 claims, and they do. I have clients who have paid long-term healthcare premiums for decades only to have the insurance company terminate those plans because they were too expensive for the firm to continue to offer.

Rarely do you see a headline about an insurance company losing money.

Entrepreneurs buy a great deal of insurance, but not solely for wealth protection. The insurance products they buy are "hybrids," designed for protection and investment. For example, variable universal life insurance can serve as both life insurance and an investment vehicle. The insurance company takes post-tax dollars as a premium and invests those deposits as tax-deferred growth. Costs on such products are high, and when you withdraw, the gains are converted and taxed at ordinary income rates rather than at lower capital gains rates.

While there are limited cases where hybrid products may serve a particular purpose, my view is that, in general, for most entrepreneurs, insurance is too expensive to be used as an investment vehicle. It has additive costs plus a legal contract. That contract might use a term like *guarantee*, but you have to read carefully to understand what that means. Often, a guarantee is valid...until it isn't. Again, it is an insurance company's job, as part of meeting their shareholders' expectations, to make sure the firm earns more than it pays out.

My belief is insurance should be purchased specifically for asset protection and risk reduction as it relates to long-term care, disability, or life circumstances, such as how David in the last chapter used insurance as part of his succession plan. Countless entrepreneurs buy hybrid insurance products from financial "advisers" who reap big commissions from the products they sell when a simpler, less costly insurance solution may be available. These advisers may not be truly helping people evaluate what kind of insurance they need.

LUCY'S STORY

Let's look at wealth protection through Lucy's planning. Lucy is a forty-year-old entrepreneur. She and her partner, Rosie, have two kids. Rosie is a stay-at-home mom; Lucy handles all the finances. Lucy is in year five of running her office staffing company. The first adviser she visited (a fee-based adviser who also sold financial products) urged her to buy an annuity for retirement. An annuity is a contract with an insurance company that will provide fixed sums to the investor, usually for rest of their life. But the second adviser Lucy visited (a fee-only one) pointed out that there were too many long-term tax disadvantages with the annuity, and the underlying expenses were two to three times as expensive as a mutual fund. With over twenty years until retirement, Lucy determined she had enough time in the stock market to let her money grow, rather than locking it up with the annuity.

Lucy decided to stick with the second adviser as she went

through the rest of the process of setting up wealth protection. She had been urged by the first adviser to buy whole life insurance, one of the hybrid investment products I previously discussed. Often called permanent insurance, whole life insurance does not expire (requiring payments from you for the rest of your life). Lucy opted instead to get a twenty-year level term insurance policy. It was a fraction of the cost of the whole life policy and had higher coverage limits. Lucy decided that she only needed life insurance for a set period of time. After twenty years, she would be sixty-two. By then, the family's debts, including the kids' college loans, would be paid off. The kids would be grown and financially independent. Lucy's business would also be fully established and secure, and at that point, Lucy could self-insure. Rosie could cover any remaining expenses after her death with money set aside from her pensions, investments, and savings.

Because Lucy decided to go with term instead of whole life insurance, she was able to afford both long-term care insurance and a disability policy. If Lucy became disabled and could not work, she would still receive $10,000 a month for her family because of the disability policy. Early-onset Alzheimer's runs in Lucy's family; her mother was diagnosed at fifty-seven. If the same thing happened with Lucy and she could no longer care for herself, the long-term care insurance would cover all her needs, including twenty-four-hour nursing care.

Lucy wanted to ensure she would never be a burden to her spouse or kids, and she wanted to protect her assets for their benefit. Having both policies gave her a great deal of peace of mind.

Lucy was concerned about an additional health issue and broached it with the second adviser. She had a history of breast cancer in her family. Her mom had had a mastectomy at age forty-five, and her sister had just been diagnosed. Lucy wanted to take additional protective measures with her finances in case she, too, got breast cancer. With her new adviser's guidance, she set up health savings and flexible spending accounts at her company. Both allow her to save for potential out-of-pocket expenses, including breast reconstruction surgery, which was not covered by her health insurance.

Finally, Lucy's new adviser alerted her that under wealth protection, she needed the right levels of insurance for her home and auto coverage. Because entrepreneurs have deep pockets, they can be the targets of lawsuits if they are in traffic accidents. In addition, a lawsuit can be filed if their children have an accident driving a vehicle while on their personal policies. Lucy ended up moving one of the personal vehicles to the company policy, which lowered her personal premiums, and she raised the limits on her personal property and casualty insurance. She also purchased an umbrella policy for additional liability protection that cost only $250 a year and doubled her personal limits.

READ INSURANCE CONTRACTS CAREFULLY

With insurance, every situation is different, and you need to examine your family history and circumstances to tailor your coverage. I want to reiterate it is imperative with any kind of policy or product that you drill down to understand the contract. With hybrid products especially, you must understand not only the contract, but also the landscape in which it is being presented. For example, let's say you have $100,000 and are concerned about putting it in the stock market. On the advice of an adviser you decide to put it into a variable indexed-annuity policy designed to protect you from market downturns. The adviser assures you that you will never take a market loss; you will always get the upside.

The way things will very likely play out is more complicated. Your product is tied to an index; for purposes of this example, I'll use the S&P 500. Your contract stipulates you get a 1 percent increase for every 1 percent increase of the S&P 500, up to a cap of either 1 percent per month or a total cap of 6 percent for the year. If you look at how the stock market really works, it does drop significantly occasionally, but it also rises significantly. You may believe 1 percent per month equals a 12 percent return. In reality, the fine print states you can only ever get 6 percent because that's the true cap. The bottom line is that actuaries have gone to great lengths to figure out statistically how much the insurance company needs to keep for itself when the market goes up (keep in mind the casino metaphor). A contract's cap can be tied to many different variables, all of which may be difficult for you to determine. You typically can't exit these policies without a stiff penalty for at least ten or twelve years, depending on the cancellation schedule. The penalty typically erases any benefit you might have achieved, and then some. Far more times than I can count, I've seen entrepreneurs realize that many of these contracts are not in their best interest. Unfortunately, that realization has come only after they've signed on the dotted line.

Many times entrepreneurs seek safety through such products. A trustworthy adviser will be able to direct you to what is truly prudent. They can see what you can't. You don't want to risk missing the opportunity to have the volatility of the market work on your behalf. You don't want to react from fear because, unfortunately, fear is the tool used to market these products. Working with an interpretive adviser will help round out a conversation. He or she will guide you to step back and ask whether such an investment is logical. A product might provide protection in a specific situation, but if such a situation is uncommon, buying that protection is a waste of resources. An adviser who has worked with hundreds of entrepreneurs and has seen multiple situations will have a far more accurate, objective perspective than one selling products outside of the fiduciary standard.

CHAPTER ELEVEN

CHARITABLE GIFTING

John and Yvonne built one of the first solar installation companies in their state. They worked night and day for years to make it successful. As their third decade in business approached, they had the opportunity to merge with a large publicly held global services firm, in effect selling their company. They planned to retire after the deal was done. They had been working with us for many years, and, in December, they came to me to finalize their plans and discuss what to do with the proceeds.

During their initial master-map discussions with us, John and Yvonne had noted that they wanted to make a difference during their retirement years. Their dream was to drive their Airstream around the United States and volunteer at different stops. They wanted to live comfortably, not extravagantly, give back, and pass some of their assets and savings on to their two sons. They wanted to be free from the financial strain they had experienced while building their business and ensure they could support themselves for the rest of their lives. Yet John and Yvonne were uncertain if they had enough money to retire well.

When they merged their company with the publicly held one, John and Yvonne received fifty thousand shares of the acquiring company's stock, in exchange for their shares in their company stock. The value of the acquiring stock had a price of sixty dollars a share. The total value of exchanged stock was $3 million, and John and Yvonne had an extremely low cost basis in their company stock. Cost basis is the original value or purchase price of the stock for tax purposes, which is used to determine the capital gain, the difference between the stock's purchase price and its current market value.

In addition, John and Yvonne received $400,000 in combined wages plus $1 million worth of stock options in the acquiring company. The wages and options would be taxed as ordinary income. The couple expected that, given their income situation post-sale, they would be in the highest federal and state tax brackets. We calculated they would owe $518,349 in taxes, something they wanted to minimize.

John and Yvonne had saved well over the years. Their

savings had been prudently diversified in their remaining portfolio. After analyzing their situation, we determined they had enough to retire on comfortably, regardless of the value of the new shares of stock. We began looking at their interest in charitable gifting as a way to reduce the risk of the future value of the options and to offset their tax bill. We devised a plan to gift 7,119 shares of stock they received in exchange for the acquiring company's stock. Their transferred cost basis in the new stock was $1 a share—anything above the basis is taxed at capital gains rates. Hence, 7,119 at $59 a share generated roughly $420,000 in charitable deductions, enough to partially offset the income that the stock options generated.

To sum up: the couple had the opportunity to partially offset the $1 million in options by gifting $420,000 in stock, and through some additional planning, save $146,520 in taxes.

John and Yvonne chose to lower their tax bill and benefit their community at the same time. They contributed $420,000 to a donor-advised fund, the philanthropic vehicle that allows donors to make a charitable contribution and receive immediate tax benefits. John and Yvonne needed time to decide which charities would receive the money, and the donor-advised fund permitted them to count the contribution on their taxes and still wait to take the time to decide how to gift the money.

Not all donor-advised funds are created equal. Many are set up by investment companies to sell their own products, with investments limited to high-cost underlying funds. But other donor-advised funds provide open platforms where the adviser can select the investments. That is the kind John and Yvonne chose, resulting in the creation of an endowment of sorts. It wasn't technically an endowment, but the money would continue to grow during their retirement years. John and Yvonne planned to involve their boys in selecting charities, turning the fund into something akin to a family foundation, one that would teach their sons about the power of philanthropy.

MAKE CHARITABLE GIFTING PART OF A STRATEGIC PLAN

Like John and Yvonne, many entrepreneurs have an inclination toward philanthropy. They feel they've worked hard, received much, and have a responsibility to give back. They usually involve their companies in community events, encourage employees to get involved in charitable organizations, and sit on nonprofit boards themselves. One of the main reasons I left my corporate career and dove into entrepreneurship was that I wanted to make a bigger impact on my community. While I deeply wanted to serve families and small businesses, I also wanted to reserve about 30 percent of my time to work on charitable projects, and I have done so. On a larger scale, global entrepreneurs like Bill Gates and Warren Buffett have set up a giving pledge that 168 billionaires have signed, formally promising to give away at least half of their wealth to philanthropic causes.

For many entrepreneurs, however, the topic of charitable gifting only pops up at the end of the year, rather than as part of a strategic wealth management and protection plan. An excellent financial adviser will make visible the ways to maximize charitable gifting's potential so your decisions can be more proactive. Sometimes all it takes is asking the question: Would you rather money that is no longer in your pocket go to the federal government or to charities? In John and Yvonne's case, they decided they would rather make the choice of what to do with the $420,000 than to lose it to taxes.

MORE WAYS TO MITIGATE TAXES

John and Yvonne's strategy is an example of using a one-time earning event and/or stock option gain to offset a tax impact. Another sound strategy is to manage your tax brackets by making periodic gifts over multiple years. For example, Jim and Layla are married and make $315,000, which puts them in the 24 percent federal tax bracket. But this year, Layla received a bonus, making their taxable income $330,000, which puts them in the 32 percent tax bracket. They decide to gift $15,000 to a donor-advised fund; by doing so, they drop to the 24 percent tax bracket, saving $4,800 in federal tax.

Again, such a strategy is definitely for those with a charitable mindset. Jim and Layla normally gave $10,000 a year to worthy causes. But when Layla received the bonus, they decided they would rather just give the $15,000 to charity. If they had not, they would have paid the $4,800 and had roughly $10,000 to give anyway. The couple plans to keep using this strategy when it's appropriate.

Looking at another strategy, many times entrepreneurs invest early in tech stocks that end up in merger situations. With a merger, there is an exchange of stock, and depending on the terms, cash may be distributed to the shareholder as well. In tax terms, the cash is called "boot," and it is taxed as ordinary income. Often, entrepreneurs gift a portion of boot to charity by donating shares of stock associated with boot, especially if they are already in a high tax bracket.

Many entrepreneurs, unfortunately, do things the way they did when they worked for a corporation: give with after-tax dollars. Maybe they give 10 percent of their paycheck a week to their church, temple, synagogue, or mosque. But they could do so much more by planning strategically and giving with pretax dollars. With a gift of appreciated stock to pay for a religious organization's membership dues, you don't pay tax on any capital gains, and you get the full deduction of the charitable contribution. If the stock cost you fifty dollars a share three years ago, and it's now worth one hundred dollars a share, gifting it is a wise way to take advantage of the return and avoid additional taxes.

THE MANY RETURNS ON GIFTS

My client Barbara's situation exemplifies another smart use of charitable gifting. Her father, Nick, was an entrepreneur who owned a pipe manufacturing business in the Midwest, and Barbara grew up doing the books and employee management. Her brothers stayed with the business after college. Barbara married and became a public school teacher. However, she continued to help with the family business when needed. When Nick and his sons received the opportunity to sell the business, Nick wanted to make sure Barbara was recognized for her contribution.

Nick sold the business to another small manufacturing company, and he agreed to take payments on the sale price over the next five years. Nick made Barbara a shareholder, so she also received a portion of those loan payments. Barbara and her husband, also a teacher, had lived a frugal lifestyle their entire lives. They had raised four children in a modest home, and the money from the sale of the family business was a windfall for them. The couple offset the income related to the loan payments by making periodic gifts on an annual basis to a donor-advised fund, which mitigated the tax impacts. They also set up educational trusts for their grandkids, segregating the assets and thus not subjecting them down the line to estate tax.

A SHIFT IN MINDSET

The tax strategies I've described all require an integration mindset. If you have a strong desire to participate in charitable gifting, your financial adviser should identify that wish and integrate it into your comprehensive plan. Perhaps gifting is something you've never considered. In that case, your adviser should provide the opportunity for you to develop an interest and benefit from it.

As in all the stories I've discussed, a charitable gift doesn't mean you don't end up paying taxes or that you don't end up with less cash after making the gift. But you get a different kind of return. Studies show charitable gifting is directly tied to greater well-being and happiness. The satisfaction of directly impacting people's lives is a gift that gives back forever.

CONCLUSION

Laurie is a tech entrepreneur who came to me because she had just gotten hit with a tax bill of $150,000, more than she had ever paid in her life. She felt frustrated with her CPA's lack of help in sheltering more of her hard-earned money from taxes. She was also overwhelmed with the demands of her business. Laurie found my practice after educating herself on the different business models in the financial services industry. She learned that brokers and fee-based advisers are not always required to act in a client's best interest, and, given the tax bill, she did not want to lose any more assets through a relationship with a financial adviser who charged high fees and commissions. By doing research on CEFEX, she realized she wanted an adviser who used the Centre's decade-long proven process of communication and implementation. She found me after searching online for a fee-only fiduciary adviser.

Like most entrepreneurs, Laurie's tax consequences had not been integrated into an overall plan, and she learned the importance of that during the master-map process.

Given Laurie's tax bracket, she was keeping 56.7 percent after taxes. She was working hard and succeeding, but keeping only about the same amount she had been making while working for a corporation. She felt like she was rowing a boat with one oar. Laurie did have an interest in a more robust set of benefits and retirement plans. I explained to her that there were costs to providing structures such as matching and profit sharing to employees, but she would still benefit even after paying for those costs. More specifically, I shifted $175,000 of Laurie's income: $7,000 went to matching and profit sharing for her employees, and $168,000 went to the shelter of a new retirement plan. That one step reduced her tax burden by half.

With the income sheltered, the next question was how eventually to pay tax on that money. I looked at a twenty-year cash flow forecast toward her expected retirement date. Then I implemented strategies that would allow her to pull that money out in retirement at a rate of 19.25 percent rather than 43.6 percent (federal and state tax combined). I also recommended Laurie implement a health savings account for herself and her family so she would never pay tax on the earnings for qualified medical expenses. She also implemented a donor-advised fund and gifted to it periodically to keep her income at a lower bracket, as well as using 529 plans to help fund her children's education. After working with me, Laurie was thrilled not only with the financial results but with the fact that she felt she had finally met an adviser who truly cared about her goals and integrated the many facets of wealth management.

DEMAND THE BEST

If you feel stuck when it comes to wealth management and planning, I'm here to assure you that is not an uncommon experience. I'd like to urge you to take the time, like Laurie did, to find an adviser who has your best interests in mind. With a trustworthy adviser, you can let go of the burden of wealth management and focus on what matters to you. Your financial well-being increases.

Such an adviser will assist you in creating a master map. In orienteering, you must figure out where you are on a master map, what the next obstacle is likely to be, and how to go around it. You must plan for checkpoints and for the end of your journey. Often, once you get on the ground, things look different than they did on the map. One section of countryside might take you through a swamp, another through a thick forest or a rock-strewn field. You won't necessarily know until you're there. Same with creating a robust financial plan. An excellent adviser will help figure out how to navigate every turn of your master map. You don't have to understand the whole course at the start.

By reading this book, I hope you've realized that without a trustworthy financial adviser and robust, well-thought-out process, the likelihood of reaching your desired destination is slim. Postponing decisions about finances can mean the difference between a retirement spent playing golf or tennis every day and one where you're forced to work at a part-time job. You can get where you want to go by remembering that the result will always reflect the process.

The wealth management arena can be overwhelming, with different types of advisers, unfamiliar terms, and the noise of the financial media and well-intended friends. The right adviser will cut through all that. It is critical to ask yourself:

- Am I getting what I need from my relationship with my financial adviser?
- Do I have a good understanding of the process he or she is using?

I hope I've helped you define what to look for in an advisory relationship, and I'd like to continue to offer you assistance and resources at www.waynebtitus3.com. I also blog regularly and offer podcasts, webinars, and educational materials at amdgservices.com. If you have questions, I'd love to hear from you. Drop me an email at info@amdgservices.com. It's my honor that you've read *The Entrepreneur's Guide to Financial Well-Being*. I appreciate you providing me with the opportunity to share this important information with you as you develop your own master map and navigate to your unique destination.

APPENDIX

HOW TO PREPARE FOR A DISCOVERY MEETING WITH YOUR ADVISER (CHAPTER 4)

A discovery meeting with your adviser is an opportunity to share information about your financial situation, communication preferences, and interests, as well as discuss your life and financial goals. Consider it a deep "getting to know you" session. At AMDG Financial, we refer to our discovery sessions as an opportunity to create a "master map" with our clients—a map we will use to support them on their journey to financial well-being.

Your adviser may ask you to bring certain documents to your first meeting. The purpose of this request is to help the adviser better understand your starting point on the master map. While having a conversation is important, allowing your adviser to review these documents may help him or her identify gaps in your financial picture, to discover opportunities to lower fees, or to pick up information you may forget to bring up during the meeting. We typically ask for:

- Tax returns from the past two years
- Recent financial statements, such as those from refinancing or other situations
- Bank statements from the past year
- Brokerage statements from the past year (If the cost basis is not included on these statements, we ask clients to request an unrealized gains and losses statement from their brokers.)
- Life insurance and annuity polices
- Employee benefit statements, including those for 401(k), 403(b), 457, pension, or other IRA or retirement plans
- Will or trust documents
- Any other documents the client believes would be useful to provide a deeper understanding of their financial situation

After scanning the original versions of each document to our secure system, we return them to the client. We also are available to answer questions if a client is unsure where to locate a particular document.

One of the purposes for a master-map meeting is to get to know a client as an individual, so don't be surprised if you are asked personal questions that may seem like they have nothing to do with money. That's because the better your adviser knows you, your lifestyle, and your interests, the better he or she can understand how you might react in situations such as a down market, an emergency with a loved one, or an opportunity in your particular area(s) of interest arising. Broadly, here are the types of personal questions you might encounter in a discovery meeting:

GOALS

- Tell me about some of your top accomplishments.
- What are your professional goals?
- What goals or successes do you have for your children, parents, spouse/significant other, or other loved ones?
- Describe how you see yourself participating financially in the world. (This could involve a favorite cause or charity.)

RELATIONSHIPS

- What family relationships are most important to you?
- Do you support any religious causes or schools? In what way?
- How important are your relationships in your community to you?
- How important are your relationships with coworkers?

ASSETS

- Do you save or set aside money to invest? If so, what is your process for earmarking those funds, and how much do you set aside?
- Do you anticipate changing the way you save or invest in the future? In what way?
- Describe your strategy for handling investments.
- What is your anticipated pension, retirement, or Social Security income?
- Describe some of your best and worst financial moves.

OTHER ADVISERS

- Do you work with an attorney, accountant, investment adviser, or financial planner now?
- How proactive are these advisers? Do they come to you with information and ideas, or do you need to request their assistance?
- Have you switched from any of these advisers recently, and if so, why?

PROCESS

- How involved do you like to be in managing your finances?
- Would you use secure, twenty-four-hour access to online statements, performance reports, tax returns, and other documents?

- How much contact do you expect with your financial adviser?

INTERESTS

- What types of sports/TV/movies/books do you prefer?
- What is your health and fitness regime?
- What are your hobbies?
- What charitable causes do you support?

You can help your adviser be more effective on your behalf if you take the time to seriously consider your answers to these questions. If you haven't thought about them before, answering questions like these may seem taxing—both from a time and emotional perspective. However, achieving clarity about what is important to you is critical to your long-term financial well-being.

There are no right or wrong answers to these questions. An excellent adviser will not judge you for your philosophy on life, your approach to managing money, your personal interests, or your relationships. The goal is to help you be successful on your terms.

CAPITAL GAINS AND DIVIDENDS (CHAPTER 7)

Capital gains and losses can generally be classified in two

ways: a short-term capital gain/loss describes an asset you hold for only a short time—in this case, one year or less. If you dispose of an asset after a year or more, it is considered to be a long-term capital gain or loss. There are exceptions to this rule, which are outlined in IRS Publications 544 and 550 (available at www.IRS.gov). Short-term gains are taxed as ordinary income, while long-term gains are taxed at a lower rate.

"Qualified dividend income" is taxed at a capital gains tax rate, which is lower than the tax rate for unqualified, or ordinary, dividends. To be considered qualified, a dividend must have been paid by a US company or a qualifying foreign company and must not be listed by the IRS as non-qualifying.

In addition, the dividend faces a holding period requirement: for common stock, an investor must hold the shares for more than 60 days during the 121-day period before what is called the "ex-dividend" date. An ex-dividend date is the date that a stock begins to trade without its dividend. For preferred stock, the holding-period requirement is more than 90 days during a 181-day period that starts 90 days before the ex-dividend date.

The unfortunate lesson for Raj was not thinking holistically about his portfolio and the tax implications of making changes. Always remember, it's not about how much you earn, it's about how much you keep after you pay taxes. Most clients of financial advisers expect their adviser to always place their interests first, but many advisers are neither experts at tax, nor incentivized to take a holistic point of view when managing their clients' assets. The result? A *caveat emptor* (buyer beware) situation for unwitting investors.

BACK-DOOR ROTH IRA CONTRIBUTIONS (CHAPTER 8)

The biggest difference you'll find between a traditional IRA and a Roth IRA has to do with taxes. With a traditional IRA, your taxes are deferred until you take a distribution. The opposite is true for a Roth IRA: you pay taxes up front—before you contribute; then your contributions grow tax-free, and when you make a withdrawal, the withdrawal is also tax-free. A traditional IRA might be a smart choice for you if you expect your tax bracket to be lower in retirement. If you think it might be higher, a Roth might be the way to go. A third option could be to hedge your bets and do both. Much depends upon your particular situation.

A back-door Roth contribution comes into play when a person with a traditional IRA (like Edie, in our example) makes too much money to be able to reap the benefits of a tax-deductible contribution. Edie and Frank are married, filing jointly. To make a tax-deductible contribution to her IRA, their modified adjusted gross income, or MAGI, would need to be $101,000 or less (assuming Frank is not working) for Edie and Frank to get the full deduction. But they can tap into the benefits of a Roth IRA by contributing to it *indirectly* (i.e. through the back door). Here's how it works:

- Frank makes a nondeductible contribution to his traditional IRA.
- He next converts the balance in the traditional IRA to a Roth IRA.

Edie and Frank need to report the original contribution and the conversion on IRS Form 8606. This is important because they need to record their "basis" (the amount of Frank's IRA contribution for which Edie and Frank have already paid taxes).

Further, Edie and Frank will have to pay taxes on any amount they convert from a pretax account to a Roth, and they may owe taxes on their back-door conversion if Frank still has money left in any other pretax IRA accounts.

Clear as mud? Here's something else to think about: if Frank's traditional IRA holds both pre- and after-tax funds, any conversion to a Roth subjects them to the IRS's *pro-rata* rule, which some people refer to as the "cream in the coffee" rule. For example, if you add cream to your coffee, the coffee and cream become mixed and there's no way to separate the two. It's the same principle when after-tax dollars go into a traditional IRA, because they're mingled with pretax dollars, and any distribution involves a mix of both.

In Edie and Frank's case, if Frank's traditional IRA held a balance of $200,000, including $20,000 in after-tax contributions, 10 percent of the balance would be after-tax. Any distribution, then, would include 90 percent pretax and 10 percent after-tax dollars. If Frank decides to withdraw $20,000 to help Edie start a new venture, the breakdown follows the same proportions—$18,000 pretax and $2,000 after-tax. The IRA account then has a new balance of $180,000, with $18,000 still considered after-tax dollars.

If Frank tries to do a Roth conversion using this account, he triggers the *pro-rata* rule. If he moves $20,000 to a Roth, the same formula is in effect, and the $18,000 then appears on the couple's tax return as taxable.

A number of other rules and exceptions apply, but you get the idea. A forward-looking adviser will identify these cream-in-the-coffee issues, propose beneficial alternatives, and create a twenty- to forty-year cash flow tax plan to help you stay on top of the tax implications for your retirement savings for the long term.

FSAS, HSAS, AND HRAS (CHAPTER 8)

You'll see these three acronyms frequently around open-enrollment time, and any adviser worth their salt should be discussing using these options if they are available. Here's the skinny on each:

FLEXIBLE SPENDING ACCOUNTS (FSAS)

Also known as Flexible Spending Arrangements, Flexible Spending Accounts may be offered by an employer in lieu of, or in addition to, a health insurance policy. As with an HSA, FSAs are funded pretax, by payroll deduction, which can lower the employee's taxable income for the year. Employers set the contribution limits for FSAs, while the specified limit for dependent care accounts is $5,000 per year. Unlike HSAs, however, FSA funds need to be used by the end of their run-out period, which is usually three months after the end of the year. Prior to the Affordable Care Act, employees who didn't use the funds in their account wound up forfeiting those funds to their employers. Be sure to review your plan's specific carryover allowance.

HEALTH SAVINGS ACCOUNTS (HSAS)

Health Savings Accounts, or HSAs, must be combined with a qualified high-deductible health insurance plan. The tax advantaged account can be used to help pay your deductible, and any funds left in your savings account earn tax-deferred interest. Your contributions to your HSA are tax deductible, and withdrawals to pay for your qualified medical expenses are tax-free. But here's the best part: the money in your account is yours to keep—you don't have to "use it or lose it" by the end of the year. Contributions are tax-deductible and if you use them for qualified medical expenses in the future, the growth and withdrawal are tax-free.

HEALTH REIMBURSEMENT ACCOUNTS (HRAS)

Many types of Health Reimbursement Accounts (also called Health Reimbursement Arrangements) exist, but we'll focus on those that are linked with high-deductible health insurance plans. Employers may offer an HRA to employees and their families who enroll in the company's group health insurance plan. An HRA differs from an HSA and FSA in that the employer is the only one who contributes, and, like an FSA, the employer owns the account. Because it is controlled by the employer, it would not be included in a wealth enhancement strategy.

The IRS offers further details on these plans and their allowable deductions. You can find the link at our website: http://www.WayneBTitus3.com/resources.

FINANCIAL SCRAPBOOKING (CHAPTER 9)

When a friend or relative faces a lengthy hospital stay, family members or trusted individuals often need to help keep the person's household running. That may mean locating insurance policies, helping to pay bills, or placing regular deliveries or services, such as housekeeping, on hold. But what if the person in the hospital is unconscious, unable to speak, or will need long-term care? That's when having a Financial Scrapbook℠ is a handy tool.

A financial scrapbook includes not only important documents and account numbers, but also information to enable someone to temporarily run a household. A scrapbook includes the following:

· What bills must be paid each month (such as mortgage and homeowner association payments, utilities, cable, telephone and internet, credit cards, etc.) with account numbers and company contact information
· Contact names and phone numbers for ongoing ancillary household services, such as grocery delivery, housecleaning, pest control, yard care, and so forth
· Pet-care directions and veterinary information
· A copy of the individual's financial plan, with a list of savings and investment accounts, along with statements for each account
· Important documents, such as birth certificates, marriage licenses, divorce decrees, car titles, property

deeds, wills, passports, medical directives, and burial plot information
- Insurance documents with account information (auto, life, health, umbrella, etc.)
- Tax returns for the past three to five years
- Log-in information for all online accounts, including social media
- Instructions on who to contact in the event of the person's death (family members, friends, attorneys, insurance agents, funeral homes, government agencies, such as the Social Security Administration—even the individual's Christmas card list)

Your Financial Scrapbook℠ should be kept in a safe place, such as a safe deposit box. The scrapbook can be in notebook form or stored on a jump drive. Let a trusted family member or friend know how to gain access to it in an emergency.

If families create a scrapbook together, it can also be an opportunity to hold important discussions around end-of-life issues. A Financial Scrapbook℠ makes it easy to locate important documents, but even more important, it makes it easy for loved ones to help during an otherwise stressful time. If you would like to create a Financial Scrapbook℠, please visit www.WayneBTitus3.com/resources for additional information.

WHY YOUR COLLEGE-AGED CHILD NEEDS A DURABLE POWER OF ATTORNEY (CHAPTER 9)

In most states, eighteen is the "age of majority," the moment when children are considered adults. At this point, teenagers assume legal control over their own medical and financial records, terminating the responsibilities of their parents or guardians. Without a simple estate plan in place for their eighteen-year-olds, parents may be surprised in an emergency when they can't access a child's accounts.

Here's a hypothetical situation: John and June sent their son, Tom, off to college. Tom and a group of friends decided to carpool home for the weekend. On the way, they got into a serious car accident that left Tom unconscious and in the hospital. Distraught, John and June called the hospital to try to learn about their son's condition, but because Tom was an adult, the hospital refused to release information about his status. When they arrived at the hospital, John and June couldn't even speak with Tom's doctor. They had to wait until Tom regained consciousness and gave his doctors permission to release his medical information to his parents.

You can imagine the heartache and frustration a parent might feel in this situation, not to mention confusion. Most parents assume that if a child still lives at home, or if they are paying to send that child to college, they still have the right to make decisions on their child's behalf.

With a simple estate plan, Tom's situation could have played out much differently. At a basic level, his plan should have included:

- A Health Insurance Portability and Accountability Act (HIPAA) release. A signed HIPAA release could have enabled doctors to release information about Tom's medical condition to his parents.
- A healthcare proxy. If Tom had a healthcare proxy in place, and had named his parents as his agent, they would have been able to make healthcare decisions on his behalf when he was unable to make those decisions on his own.
- Financial power of attorney. If Tom had remained unconscious for months and had given financial power of attorney to his parents, John and June would have been able to access Tom's bank accounts, pay his bills, and speak to his landlord about his apartment lease.

Beyond the basics, and perhaps as Tom gets older, he could consider keeping a list of all of his social media accounts and subscriptions (including log-in information) and naming a trusted individual to manage or terminate those accounts in the event of his death. In addition, Tom might consider creating a basic will or purchasing a life insurance policy that would cover his burial expenses. He should also think about identifying beneficiaries for his bank accounts or his 401(k) when he gets his first job. Finally, he should revisit his estate plan regularly, because a young person's life changes frequently.

ACKNOWLEDGMENTS

At AMDG Financial, our vision is that our commitment to the highest level of stewardship principles will result in the overall well-being of our community. We define "our community" as our clients and their families; our team members and their families; our business partners; and our local and international community.

This book would not have been possible without both the opportunity to serve our community and the support we have received from it.

To that end, I'd like to specifically acknowledge and thank the following people:

My wife and best friend, Lisa—for your work over the years in our businesses (your contribution is bigger than you give yourself credit for) and for challenging, supporting, and loving me in our great journey of life together.

My children, Wayne IV and David, and their wives, Em and Caley—for your good-natured ribbing. Thank you for the hilarious skit for my fiftieth birthday regarding my use of the "F" word (fiduciary) and for the number of fiduciary gold stamps on our business door (there are none...).

My business partners, Becky and Ramey—Becky for your hard work and patience in helping me build and operate my practice from the very beginning; Ramey for your insight and guidance in communicating our messages and your role in helping me bring this book to fruition.

My entire AMDG Services family—Michele, Kim, Chris, Luke, Mary, Mark, and Ken—for your dedication and hard work, and for helping me to feel free enough to write this book. I look forward to our continuing journey together.

My parents, Wayne and Sandy—for your encouragement and inspiration to always be trustworthy and to do the right thing.

Jules, fellow CPA and Rotarian—for your thoughts as I composed my initial outline.

Don Trone—for your influence (before we ever even met)

regarding procedural prudence and the recognition that prudent process provides opportunities for better investment outcomes for our clients, and for your continued work assisting us in identifying and training effective leaders for AMDG Financial.

Atul Gawande—for writing *The Checklist Manifesto*. Reading it inspired and helped me to make the complex simple.

And especially my clients—for the trust you place in us, the opportunity to serve you and your families over the years, and for sharing the rich and sacred content of your lives and your dreams.

ABOUT THE AUTHOR

WAYNE TITUS lives outside of Detroit with his wife, Lisa. They have two sons—Wayne, an account executive with a large chemical manufacturing company, and David, a chemical engineer who works in appliance manufacturing.

Wayne is committed to being a lifelong learner in countless areas, whether that's studying beekeeping, a new diet and exercise regimen, conversational Spanish, or the history of the Civil War. He is also highly involved in his community. As a district governor of Rotary International, he spent a year visiting the fifty-two clubs in his district and leading 1,600 Rotarians. He volunteers with the Michigan Association of CPAs as chair of the Financial Literacy Task Force, which helps educate the public and improve overall financial literacy, and as chair of the Individual Income Tax Study group, which educates businesses and entrepreneurs about recent tax law changes. Wayne also spends a significant amount of his time contributing to charitable enterprises, including international clean water projects with Rotary.